THE BEST OF
BALTIMORE BEAUTIES PART II

More Patterns for Album Blocks

Elly Sienkiewicz

C&T PUBLISHING

© 2002 by Elly Sienkiewicz
Editor: Cyndy Lyle Rymer
Technical Editor: Karyn Hoyt-Culp
Copyeditor/Proofreader: Laura Reinstatler/Emily Hopkins
Cover Designer: Kristen Yenche
Design Director/Book Designer: Kristen Yenche and Tim Manibusan
Illustrator: Jeffrey Carillo
Production Assistant: Tim Manibusan
Photography: Sharon Risedorph unless otherwise noted
Published by C&T Publishing, Inc., P.O. Box 1456, Lafayette,
California 94549

Front cover: "Theorem Style Urn of Fruit", New Pattern #10
Back cover: "Square Wreath of Embroidered Flowers", New Pattern #8,
"Baltimore Basket of Roses", New Pattern #6, "Heart Wreath of Acorns",
New Pattern #2

Attention Copy Shops: Please note the following exception—Publisher and
author give permission to photocopy up to three copies of all pages for
personal use only.

Attention Teachers: C&T Publishing, Inc. encourages you to use this book as a
text for teaching. Contact us at 800-284-1114 or www.ctpub.com for more
information about the C&T Teachers Program.

We take great care to ensure that the information included in this book is
accurate and presented in good faith, but no warranty is provided nor results
guaranteed. Since we have no control over the choices of materials or
procedures used, neither the author nor C&T Publishing, Inc. shall have any
liability to any person or entity with respect to any loss or damage caused
directly or indirectly by the information contained in this book.

Trademarked (™) and Registered Trademark (®) names are used throughout
this book. Rather than use the symbols with every occurrence of a trademark
and registered trademark name, we are using the names only in the editorial
fashion and to the benefit of the owner, with no intention of infringement.

Library of Congress Cataloging-in-Publication Data

Sienkiewicz, Elly.
  The best of Baltimore beauties : 95 patterns for album blocks and
borders / Elly Sienkiewicz.
      p. cm.
Includes index.
  ISBN 1-57120-149-1 (paper trade)
  1. Appliqué—Patterns. 2. Album quilts—Maryland—Baltimore.
  3. Patchwork—Patterns. I. Title.
  TT779 .S5424 1999
  746.46'041—dc21
                          99-050545

Published by C&T Publishing, Inc.
P.O. Box 1456
Lafayette, California 94549

Printed in China
10 9 8 7 6 5 4 3 2 1

Contents

 Lyre Floral Fruit Album Wreath Birds Basket Border Heart

Papercut Vase Music Cornucopia House Ship Frame Tree Fleur-De-Lis

GLOSSARY 9

PREFACE 11

INTRODUCTION 16

BALTIMORE ALBUM QUILTS

PATTERN 1   Fleur-de-Lis Medallion I 19

PATTERN 2   Fleur-de-Lis II 20

PATTERN 4   Betty Alderman's Scherenschnitte 21

PATTERN 5   Sylvia's Wycinanki 22

PATTERN 6   Hearts and Swans I and II 23

PATTERN 7   Rose of Sharon II 24

PATTERN 8   Folk Art Flower Wheel 25

PATTERN 10   Red Vases and Red Flowers 26

PATTERN 11   Victorian Favorite 27

PATTERN 14   Fleur-de-Lis with Rosebuds IV 28

PATTERN 15   Grapevine Wreath II 29

PATTERN 16   Strawberry Wreath II 30

PATTERN 18   Circular Sprays of Flowers 31

PATTERN 21   Fleur-de-Lis Medallion II 32

PATTERN 24   Rose Cornucopias 34

PATTERN 30   Vase with Fruits and Flowers 36

PATTERN 41   Victorian Basket of Flowers IV 38

PATTERN 42   Victorian Basket V with Fruits and Flowers 42

PATTERN 44   Scalloped Epergne of Fruit 46

Contents *(continued)*

BALTIMORE BEAUTIES AND BEYOND, Volume II

PATTERN 1   Hans Christian Andersen's Danish Hearts 50

PATTERN 7   Heart Medallion Frame 51

PATTERN 8   Goose Girl Milking 53

PATTERN 9   Hearts and Hands in a Feather Wreath 54

PATTERN 12   Wreaths of Hearts I and II 56

PATTERN 13   Bird in a Fruit Wreath 58

PATTERN 15   Goose Girl 62

PATTERN 16   Waterfowling 66

PATTERN 17   Tropical Boating 70

PATTERN 21   The Peony Border 74

DIMENSIONAL APPLIQUÉ

PATTERN 7   Rick Rack Roses 76

PATTERN 8   Flower-Wreathed Heart II 78

PATTERN 9   Lovely Lane's Grapevine Wreath 80

PATTERN 11   Basket of Quarter Roses and Buds 82

PATTERN 12   Unadorned Victorian Basket of Flowers 84

PATTERN 14   Folk Art Basket of Flowers 86

PATTERN 15   Apples in the Late Afternoon 90

PATTERN 16   Ivy Basket with Bow 94

PATTERN 17   Jeannie's Iris, Pansy, and Pleated Flowers Basket 98

PATTERN 18   Regal Bird Amidst the Roses 102

PATTERN 21   Baltimore Bouquet 106

PATTERN 27   Pedestal Basket with Handle 110

PATTERN 28   Annie Tuley's Pleated Basket 110

PATTERN 33   Kaye's Ribbon Basket 111

PATTERN 32   Ribbonwork Basket for Broiderie Perse Blooms 111

Two Borders 112, 121

Color Section 113–120

Contents *(continued)*

PAPERCUTS AND PLENTY

PATTERN 1   Kangaroos . . . . ✦ ❧ ❁ 122

PATTERN 2   Varietal Fleur-de-Lis I . . . . ✦ ❧ ❁ 122

PATTERN 5   Varietal Botanical I . . . . ✦ ❧ ❁ 123

PATTERN 6   Varietal Fleur-de-Lis II . . . . ✦ ❧ ❁ 123

PATTERN 7   Varietal Fleur-de-Lis III . . . . ✦ ❧ ❁ 124

PATTERN 8   Varietal Botanical II . . . . ✦ ❧ ❁ 124

PATTERN 9   Varietal Botanical III . . . . ❧ ✦ 125

PATTERN 10   Varietal Botanical IV . . . . ❧ ✦ 125

PATTERN 15   Varietal Fleur-de-Lis IV . . . . ✦ ❧ ❁ 126

PATTERN 16   Varietal Botanical V . . . . ✦ ❧ ❁ 126

PATTERN 17   Varietal Botanical VI . . . . ❧ ✦ 127

PATTERN 18   Varietal Botanical VII . . . . ❧ ✦ 127

PATTERN 19   Hearts and Swans . . . . ✦ ♥ ➤ 128

PATTERN 20   Abstract Design I . . . . ✦ ♥ ➤ 128

PATTERN 23   Varietal Botanical VIII . . . . ❧ ✦ 129

PATTERN 24   Varietal Botanical IX . . . . ❧ ✦ 129

PATTERN 27   Varietal Botanical X . . . . ✦ 130

PATTERN 28   Abstract Design II . . . . ✦ 130

PATTERN 29   Varietal Fleur-de-Lis V . . . . ❧ ✦ 131

PATTERN 30   Varietal Botanical XI . . . . ❧ ✦ 131

PATTERN 31   Varietal Fleur-de-Lis VI . . . . ✦ ❧ ❁ 132

PATTERN 32   Varietal Botanical XII . . . . ✦ ❧ ❁ 132

PATTERN 35   Pineapple . . . . ✦ ♉ 133

PATTERN 36   Alex's Cats . . . . ✦ ♉ 133

PATTERN 39   Varietal Fleur-de-Lis VII . . . . ✦ ❧ ❁ 134

PATTERN 40   Varietal Botanical XIII . . . . ✦ ❧ ❁ 134

PATTERN 45   Turtle Hill . . . . ♉ ⊞ ✦ 135

PATTERN 47   Carnations . . . . ⊕ ❧ ♥ 136

PATTERN 48   Double Hearts . . . . ✦ ❧ ♥ 136

Contents *(continued)*

PATTERN 49   Rose Medallion 137

PATTERN 50   Great Grandma May Ross Hamilton's Scottish Thistle 137

PATTERN 53   Hearts and Tulips 138

PATTERN 54   Landon Bears Football Team 138

PATTERN 57   Pinecones for Maine 139

PATTERN 58   Varietal Botanical XIV 139

PATTERN 59   Christmas Cactus Variation 140

PATTERN 60   Varietal Botanical XV 140

PATTERN 61   Varietal Fleur-de-Lis VIII 141

PATTERN 62   Varietal Fleur-de-Lis IX 141

PATTERN 63   Sometimes Take Tea 142

PATTERN 64   Violins and Bows 142

PATTERN 65   Flamingos 143

PATTERN 66   Eiffel Tower 143

PATTERN 67   Lindsay as a Young Gymnast 144

PATTERN 68   Family Pets 145

PATTERN 69   Tiptoe Through My Tulips 146

PATTERN 70   Ruched Ribbon Rose Lyre II 147

PATTERN 71   Cornucopia III 149

PATTERN 73   Strawberry Wreath III 153

PATTERN 74   Dove and Lyre 157

PATTERN 75   Album in a Rose Lyre Wreath 161

PATTERN 77   Victorian Basket of Flowers III 164

PATTERN 78   Basket of Full-Blown Roses 168

PATTERN 80   Half-Wreath of Blooms from Mrs. Mann's Quilt 172

PATTERN 82   Red Bird on a Passion Flower Branch 176

PATTERN 83   Folk Art Bird 180

Contents *(continued)*

NEW PATTERNS

PATTERN 1   Heart Wreath of Roses . . . . ❂ ♥ 🌷 184

PATTERN 2   Heart Wreath of Acorns. . . . . ❂ ♥ 🌷 186

PATTERN 3   Heart Wreath of Cherries . . . . ❂ ♥ 🍒 188

PATTERN 4   Heart Wreath of Tulips . . . . ❂ ♥ 🌷 190

PATTERN 5   Baltimore Rose Bouquet. . . . . ❂ 🕊 🌷 192

PATTERN 6   Baltimore Basket of Roses . . . . 🌺 🌷 🕊 196

PATTERN 7   Baltimore Urn of Roses . . . . 🏆 🌷 198

PATTERN 8   Squared Wreath of Embroidered Flowers. . . . . ❂ 🌷 200

PATTERN 9   Intertwined Crown of Flowers . . . . 🌷 201

PATTERN 10   Theorem-Style Urn of Fruit . . . . 🍒 🏆 205

PATTERN 11   Grape-Flanked Urn of Fruit. . . . . 🏆 🍒 209

PATTERN 12   Theorem-Style Urn of Flowers . . . . 🌷 🏆 213

PATTERN NOTE CONTINUATIONS 217

INDEX 219

ABOUT THE AUTHOR 224

*M*y grateful thanks to those who contributed their time
and talent to this work: The fine folks at C&T Publishing
who turned a manuscript into this book; my
friends and colleagues who thoughtfully answered
the question of why we still so love Baltimore's old Albums; and
the needleartists whose stitched beauties grace its color pages.
And thank you, dear husband, for all that you do and are.

Glossary

Album: An anthology or collection.

Album Quilt: A quilt that frames a collection of blocks on a theme.

Baltimore Album Quilts: An historic quilt style (ca.1843–1855) characterized by a collection of different blocks set together in a grid design. The blocks are appliquéd (punctuated, though rarely, by a pieced star) and are comprised of botanical blocks, picture blocks of people, places, and things, and an intentional symbolism. Their iconography underscores the impassioned nature of great numbers of these quilts having been made within a circumscribed period in the neighborhood of Baltimore City, Maryland.

Baltimore Beauties and Beyond, Studies in Classic Album Quilt Appliqué: A series of eleven books by Elly Sienkiewicz fueling the current Baltimore Album Revival. They explore the question of who made these quilts and why. In addition these books teach the contemporary quiltmaker the necessary techniques to replicate the old Albums and innovative methods for taking the style beyond Baltimore. A twelfth book on the Baltimores is actually Elly's first, self-published book, *Spoken Without a Word, 24 Faithfully Reproduced Baltimore Album Quilt Patterns with a Lexicon of Symbols* (1983).

Baltimore Beauties® for P & B Textiles: Elly Sienkiewicz's designer fabric series based on antique textiles.

Baltimore Album Revival: A period of renewed, heightened interest in understanding, collecting, and quiltmaking in the style of the mid-nineteenth century Baltimore Album Quilts. The Baltimore Museum of Art's 1981–82 exhibition of antique Baltimore Album Quilts gave the impetus to this revival which, for the third decade, is taking place in the world's industrialized countries.

Classic: of the highest quality, serving as a standard for all time.

Dr. William Rush Dunton (1868–1966): Author of *Old Quilts*; an early scholar on the Baltimore Album Quilts who left his notebooks containing a wealth of information on both the Album Quilts and early to mid-twentieth century quilt professionals to the Baltimore Museum of Art.

Fraternal Order: A society of men associated in brotherly union for mutual aid or benefit. Multiple fraternal orders flourished in eighteenth and nineteenth century America. The Oddfellows in particular burgeoned during the Baltimore Album Quilt period, showing a spectacular 500,000 candidates initiated between 1821 and 1861. A man could belong to multiple fraternal orders mid-century and one sees Oddfellow (and Rebekah), Masonic, fraternal firemen, and other orders in the antique Baltimores. The Museum of Our National Heritage in Lexington, Massachusetts provides a fine library for those interested in researching fraternal orders.

Maryland Institute for the Promotion of the Mechanic Arts: Institution where Baltimore Album Quilts were hung on exhibition at the annual fairs, held each Autumn from 1848–56. Catalogues for these exhibits list the names of those who made and deposited the quilts. Catalogues can be found at the Library of Congress, the Library of the Maryland Historical Society, and elsewhere.

Odd Fellow or Oddfellow: A member of a benevolent society that originated in England (1785–95) and spawned an American branch (begun in Baltimore by Englishman John Wildey 1830–40). Greatly expanded, it separated in 1842 from the English Order, becoming the Independent Order of Oddfellows also known in the nineteenth century as the Three-Linked Brotherhood. The three-linked chain was emblematic of their motto, "Friendship, Love, and

Truth." These links occur often in Baltimore's Albums, sometimes as chains, sometimes as the links forming a cornucopia. Victorian color symbology offers a heightened meaning for the Albums' color schemes. It is likely, for example, that the linked cornucopias of yellow (for friendship), red (for love), and blue (for truth) symbolized for the Oddfellows the blessings we are given by God. Baskets woven of the same colors seem to have been the Rebekah symbol for the same.

Oddfellows Monitor and Guide: This Oddfellow membership manual underwent several nineteenth century republications, each containing a lexicon (illustrated by engraved images) of the symbols which represented the Oddfellow and Rebekah moral precepts. The Museum of Our National Heritage library has many resources in which to pursue the Album Quilts' wealth of iconography. From linked Oddfellowdom's chains, to urns, to Rebekah doves, to hearts pierced by arrows, to cornucopias and fountains, roses and bee hives, the image—as though a pattern for a quilt block motif—and its meaning are given.

Quilt: A bed cover made of a top and bottom fabric sandwiching a filler, decoratively stitched through the three layers and bound around its outer edge.

Rebekah (Rebecca): A wife or daughter of an Oddfellow. The Rebekah degree recipients formed the Oddfellow Ladies' Auxiliary. The first Rebekah lodge opened in Baltimore (Fels Point) in 1851. If one were to graph all the documented dates inked on Baltimore Album Quilts, the bell curve peaks at 1851–52. The making of a significant number of the Album blocks may well reflect young women witnessing the Order's precepts. They may well have been contributing their time and talent to a fund-raising effort (for the order and its good works) through the making of basted block kits. The number of pumper trucks bespeaks a similar effort pursued by the various fire companies' ladies auxiliaries.

Revival: *A reawakening, a renewed interest in and care for.* The current Baltimore Album Revival can be said to have begun in the early 1980s concurrently with the Baltimore Museum of Art's exhibition of antique Baltimore Album Quilts. This exhibit hung at the Museum of Fine Arts, Houston; the Metropolitan Museum of Art, NYC; and was concluded at the Baltimore Museum of Art in Baltimore in 1982. It was accompanied by a fine full-color catalogue called *Baltimore Album Quilts* by Dena Katzenburg. *Spoken Without a Word, A Lexicon of Symbols from the Baltimore Album Quilts with 24 Faithfully Reproduced Patterns*, was published in 1983 by Elly Sienkiewicz and followed in 1989 by *Baltimore Beauties and Beyond, Volume I*, the first of an eleven book series on making these quilts. Widely disseminated among quiltmakers, these books successfully taught significant numbers of moderns to make the Baltimore-style Albums once again.

Revivalist Baltimore Album: Revivalist Baltimore Albums began to be made in the 1980s. By the time of C &T Publishing's 1994 Baltimore Album Revival Contest it was apparent that the classic style had been mastered both in the U.S. and abroad. In the best examples these Baltimore-style Albums rival their antique antecedents. Stellar quilts in that 1994 exhibition included work by hand and by machine. *Baltimore Album Revival* is the show catalog that pictures many of these innovative quilts. Their innovation was both in the blocks and in the sets. An even more magnificent blossoming was witnessed by C&T's 1998 *Baltimore Album Legacy* show with a catalogue of the same name. The revival continues, fueled by enthusiastic ranks of beginners and needleartists who, having begun the Album journey some time ago, are continuing on to make multiple Revivalist Baltimores.

Symbol: A visible sign of something invisible. A material object representing something immaterial.

Preface

Twenty Years into the Baltimore Album Revival

In Baltimore's venerable Albums, you and I, dear reader, have much in common. Two decades ago, I looked my first "Old One" in the eye. It was 1982 and she and two dozen Album sisters hung at exhibition in the Baltimore Museum of Art. The viewing took me by surprise, moved me to the edge of tears. I was a young mother: stretched, exhilarated, tired. Later I felt I'd looked into the makers' souls and, touched by fingers long stilled, I—all unsuspecting—was thereby transformed. Quickly captive, I drafted antique Album block patterns, intent upon sharing their once again fresh beauty by book (*Spoken Without a Word*). Inspired, I sought to replicate blocks seen on exhibition. It was an education in appliqué, in understanding another's soul, in sum, a joy. Baltimore's classic Album Quilt style, revisited by you and me, is evolving—like a beloved daughter—she is recognizably her mother's child, but with striking characteristics of her own.

Impassioned, I learned the style and wrote twelve books about the Albums. I was in thrall to their beauty, consumed by their mystery, mesmerized by the historical evidence so rewarding to research. My appreciation verges on the mystical. I'm fascinated by how this art can bridge life's stages. I myself—who was a young mother when I wrote my first book on the Albums—am now a mother of adults, wrestling with change, with children marrying, two become one, geographically far removed; a grandmother blessed by grandchildren too seldom seen.

The old Albums are a compass and a refuge. I stitch for peace and community. I stitch for beauty. I stitch for challenge. I stitch to have a world still my own, now that youngsters who need me no longer fill my home. New avenues beg exploration: There are more needlearts to learn—from papercuts to silhouettes, from dimensional appliqué to theorem stenciling, from ink embellishment to stuffed work and embroidery. The Albums thrill me still.

Baltimore stitching, I believe, is a meditative process by which one can reconcile that which made us what we are with both the present and the future. Through Album work, I feel connected to women in all ages, everywhere, but especially to my heroines, the good ladies of bygone Baltimore. Documents record that they showed their Album Quilts at the annual "Maryland Institute for the Promotion of the Mechanic Arts" fairs.[1] While women of that day were not yet citizens, and thus not Institute members, their handiwork hung from the 10-foot wide balconies edging the exhibition hall. In 1850, a lawyer, one Campbell Morfit, stood amidst that grandeur and lauded Baltimore's women in his opening address. Two years into the Institute's existence, his words reflect a popular hunger now, for the Institute and its members to share moral and spiritual values, to further bind them into the kind of community to which people pledge their deepest loyalty. When he speaks of society and of women's role in this community it has become metaphorical, and is couched as almost a mythical worldview.

"Society," he intones, "wants all its members to be of the most enlightened kind, and wants them all in close community. The better part of it stands like a beacon, showing its light for the haven where all may enter…

Writers upon the moral economy of nations have traced much of the greatness of their great men, and most of their highest principles, to the influence of their women—to women —to mothers, whose fine perception of natural religion and instinctive inclination to right have laid the foundation in their children of their chief stock of morals. This is no doubt true. They are the fountains, the very sources of virtue, and when to this is added the advantage of good education, they become omnipotent in their influences. Their control is not ephemeral—it dies not with the day— it passes not with their own generation, but descends, like a heavenly heritage, through many ages."

The Baltimore Album Quilts (BAQs) have indeed descended like a heavenly heritage and you and I are the most appreciative heirs.

A MINI-REVIVAL WITHIN THE REVIVAL

Oh, what a journey we have embarked upon! This Baltimore Album Revival has just greeted its third decade. Baltimore's historic beauty, rejuvenated, intrigues us and salves our spirits. Teachers and shop owners note a new revival within this decades-long revival, citing great numbers of beginners sojourning with Album appliqué. Some of these beginners look so young—and I smile, realizing they are me at that age. But why Baltimore-style Albums? They are beautiful, no question. But the world is full of beautiful quilts. Why did these particular quilts so catch our hearts so that early in the 1980s a Baltimore Revival began? Four quilt-makers who have become my friends through Album study, consider these questions:

1. What is causing a renewed revival?

"I would compare the mini-Baltimore revival to the echoes of the Baby Boom. Appliqué artists who have completed, or nearly completed, in my case, their "first Baltimore" are teaching and mentoring the next generation."—*Susan Day*

"As we have become more proficient at appliqué techniques and symbolism we can tell stories and memorialize events. One's enthusiasm to create a personal treasure is difficult to keep silent. That love of symbolism, history, and beauty is shared every time a block appears. Passion shared, passed along, and implanted firmly in one's soul—I believe it is a wish and a dream for recognition—signifying to the future that each of us was here and mattered."
—*Bette Augustine*

"I feel the current revival is occurring because Baltimore Album quilts are timeless classics. Regardless of current fads or trends, we always return to the classic form because it gives us a

foundation. Baltimore Album quilts are the "elite" of the quilt world, the standard to which we aspire."—*Ronda McAllen*

"More than a decade after it began, new quilters see the results of this Baltimore Album Revival and are drawn in. The beauty, strong colors, and demanding techniques call to those tired of the "disposable" technological world in which we live. They see quilts that are revered still, after more than 150 years, and yearn to create something with that potential for longevity."
—*Nancy Kerns*

2. Why have the BAQs caught the hearts and minds, the fancy and devotion of so many modern women? What is it about the quilts, about the women?

"The historical, societal, and floral symbolism adds an element of intrigue, inviting the modern quilter to add her own symbols to the lexicon, such as a NASA shuttle in a papercut motif. For me, the opportunities, accomplishments, and mobility achievable today have resulted in a certain rootlessness and restlessness. Studying BAQs and appliqué techniques ties me to a specific time and place, however temporarily."—*Susan Day*

"The makers of nineteenth-century album quilts had the ability to transcend the beauty of nature into a spiritual realm never before nor ever again seen in the quilt world. The quilts speak to us from a much deeper level than that of just beauty: They speak to our souls. With rich symbolism, they touch our hearts and speak to our basic beliefs in a greater power…To look inward into one's own heart, to draw from one's life experiences, and then to create something so beautiful is truly a spiritual experience."
—*Ronda McAllen*

"In a fast-paced, stress-filled world, modern women try to squeeze in some time for themselves. They choose many outlets and quilting is a growing choice. I think this style's appeal is its personal expression and the hope of creating a generation-spanning gift. I find students also get a self-esteem boost when they master these age-old techniques. Women of today crave the skills and talents of the past, and this style of quilting gives them a goal to strive for in their search for old-fashioned quality."–*Nancy Kerns*

3. How long have you been on a Baltimore Album Revival journey? Where are you in that journey and what keeps you at it?

"In 1994, I took my first workshop with Elly. From that point, I started using the same background fabric for all my Baltimore block classes, so that by 1999, I had enough to complete a full-size medallion top. I have attended The Elly Sienkiewicz Appliqué Academy® every year since the first, in 1996. What keeps me coming back are my companions on the journey: the excellent teachers and the many like-minded friends I have made."–*Susan Day*

"My Baltimore Album journey began in 1990 with a class taught by Elly at my local guild. It was a turning point. I actually realized this at that time. This is what I had been searching for—to strive for the skills to make this style quilt. These quilts spoke to me on a level I did not understand. It was a very strong pull! The result was a twenty-five block traditional Baltimore style appliqué quilt that I consider my masterpiece. I plan to make as many more, all different, as I am able….This style of quiltmaking is my favorite to teach as well. The students are awed, slightly nervous about their ability to succeed. I get great satisfaction when they are pleased with their results, and with the special techniques they have learned."–*Nancy Kerns*

"My passion for the Baltimore style surprised me. It began quietly. My sister introduced me to those curious looking, colorful, and meticulous Baltimore quilts. While she was instantly attracted to them, I viewed them in amazement, marveling that anyone would spend the time to create such massive and complex pieces. A cursory look to please her was all I could muster. But, I was per-suaded to attend an Elly Sienkiewicz lecture, and just like that, the pilgrimage began! Although it has been six years since my initial exposure to the Baltimore style, I consider myself a novice. I have been privileged to meet so many other like-minded travelers along the way. I hope someday to complete my own masterpiece of family, and perhaps world, history to pass down to my loved ones—complete with a written record of my private Baltimore Album Revival journey."
–*Bette Augustine*

"I have been on the Baltimore Album journey for five years. I feel like just a babe but what intrigues me most is not only the quilts themselves but the women who made them. I feel I cannot fully appreciate or understand these quilts unless I know the women behind them. I am now studying the social history of the Baltimore area, and through my genealogy work I am attempting to trace the descendents of some of these women to learn more about their lives."
–*Ronda McAllen*

Unanswered Questions

In previous *Baltimore Beauties* books I wove a tapestry of historic influences, both political and cultural, reflected in the Albums. Recent research confirms the picture those books painted so broadly. This research may also provide a missing puzzle piece, an answer to this question: Given the fact that appliquéd Albums reflect major cultural influences; that they proliferated within a definable timeframe (roughly from the early 1840s to the mid–1850s); and further, that certain cultural influences common to Baltimore seemed to spread geographically well beyond the environs of Baltimore; what was the conduit of transmission for this Album Phenomenon? What *mechanism of popularization*, what *vector*, to use the scientist's term, spread this challenging quilt genre and impassioned so many quiltmakers? What sustained their devotion for years? What caused this style's burgeoning numbers and its geographical spread far beyond Baltimore City?

Finding a tidy "keystone" answer is not easy. Some measure of the difficulty would be to assign causality to the Revivalist Album phenomenon that brings you and me together in this book. While the jury has only just begun to meet on that one, I hypothesize three conduits of cultural transmission for the antebellum Baltimore phenomenon. Together these conduits may so have fanned old Baltimore's fancywork fire that, revived, it again consumes us women of the industrialized world. Given the organizational structure and social concerns of mid-nineteenth century Baltimore, I argue in my lectures that the Album Quilt style spread on the wings of three institutions: the Methodist Church, the Oddfellows, and the Maryland Institute for the Promotion of the Mechanic Arts. Additionally, I would caution against the impetus to ascribe specific authorship to particular designers when supporting evidence is inadequate.

Within the current revival, two artist/major designer theories have been published, each in books eloquent with cultural history. Dena Katzenberg proposed the "Mary Evans" designer theory in the museum catalogue, *Baltimore Album Quilts*. Troubled by her conclusions, though, I questioned that theory in a paper presented to the American Quilt Study Group and later published in *Baltimore Beauties and Beyond, Vol. II*. While the fashion of crediting Mary Evans faded, another Mary has become widely cited in art and antique publications. Jennifer Goldsborough, in the museum catalogue *Baltimore Album Legacy*, names Mary Simon as a significant designer, quoting as evidence a fragmentary reference from Hannah Mary Trimbell's 2/10/1850 diary entry: "…then out to Mrs. Simon's in Chesnut (sic) St, the lady who cut & basted these handsome quilts—saw some pretty squares."[2] I am skeptical of this attribution partly because of the modesty of this evidence (a cutter/baster can be a technician only and is not necessarily a style's designer). Then, too, evidence from the current Baltimore

Album Revival shows how design innovation by one maker influences many others, so that knowledge of who the original innovator was is easily lost. Baltimore-style Album making is today, as it most probably was back then, a living and evolving style, based on the work and creativity of many, not of a famous few. Addressing the opening assembly of the first annual exhibition of the Maryland Institute, October, 1848, one John H.B. Latrobe, Esq., struck this same chord. His words describe the antebellum Album Era. Could they not explain contemporary quiltmaking institutions as well?

"Institutions like this operate in two ways," Latrobe began. "While they improve art, they improve the artizan [sic]. While they facilitate and perfect the labor of the hands, they call into action, rouse up and make active, the labor of the brain. And this last is truly their noblest function. The work of the hands…has the common fate of all human creations: but thought is imperishable, and once developed, expressed and illustrated, lives forever."

In alternating guises of philosopher, historian, and preceptor, John Latrobe seems at his finest in the role which struck me as the oratorical athletic coach. As though team members, I imagined the rising ambitions of his audience's quiltmaking women as they heard this "coach's" inspiring words:

Invention is an ancestor with a mighty progeny. First comes the crude idea—perhaps in itself a blessing to mankind. Then come the many processes by which it may be carried out, each in its turn a novelty; then come improvements on these processes; then improvements on improvements, until the original thought, the first invention—with its countless ramifications may be likened to the Indian tree, whose branches, rooting their extremities in the ground produce new trees, with like powers of reproduction, until a mighty forest stands around the parent stem. Such has been the case…in America; and the inventive genius of the people,…one of their admitted characteristics,…cannot better be accounted for, than…by the union of intellect and manual labor.[3]

Putting the history and the stitching of revivalist Baltimores into perspective, Nancy Kerns writes, "I don't know if many ladies start their journeys actually thinking about the ones who made the quilts in the past. I think it is more that they are drawn to these quilts because of the classic, enduring beauty and general appeal. As they progress, however, I think that the symbolism in the quilts excites the modern women's interest in those original stitchers and encourages them to incorporate some modern symbolism into their work. It is the common thread…a continuance of the past, with current meaning." Or, as Mr. Latrobe wrote so long ago, 'the union of intellect with the work of the hands.' Ronda McAllen concludes, "Even though these quiltmakers hail from a different time and place, they were women just like we, whose love of beauty and grace transformed and fulfilled their lives. It brought them together in a sisterhood and provided them emotional support in troubling times. As modern quilters, the Baltimore Album Quilts do the same for us."

I write this in our nation's capital, three days after September 11's plane attacks assassinated more than 3,000 innocents in less than two hours time. Though that day I stood close enough to the Pentagon to hear the bomb-like roar, feel the ground shake me from body to soul, and, later, smell bitterness borne on acrid smoke; my imagination is not big enough to encompass what happened. In time, though, I and others will stitch a square for our Albums, witness to this infamy, witness to the blessing of living in the Land of the Free. This square I'll stitch in thanksgiving for the forefathers and mothers who gave us, it turns out, enduring values and thus courage. In my mind, my block is a hero's laurel crown cradling Old Glory, symbol of our land's devotion to Liberty—Liberty, that defining American ideal of political, economic, and religious freedom. I want my block to include a burning candle for the indominability of our American dream and for the immortality of those souls sacrificed on a pyre because some so feared the strength of Freedom's promise.

Elly Sienkiewicz
Washington, DC
September 14, 2001

---

[1] From 1848-56, The Maryland Institute for the Promotion of the Mechanic Arts held annual Autumn fairs in Baltimore City. The Library of Congress and the Maryland Historical Society's Library (among others) house their catalogues, broadsides, and pamphlets. The catalogues contain invaluable evidence about the fairs (including member lists and who brought what to be shown on exhibition.) Baltimore's Album Quilts are in the listings along with the maker's and depositors names and locale. The *Baltimore Sun* newspaper lists people who won prizes and those who judged the shows. Documents are available and underutilized. To one willing to work hard, researching them promises to be most rewarding! I hope you'll share your findings in print.

[2] Goldsborough, J., *Lavish Legacies*, p 16-17. The reference's original document is in the Maryland Historical Society Library and contains overwritten words, confusing the diarist's intended meaning.

[3] Archival pamphlet in the Libary of Congress: *Addresses Delivered Before the Maryland Institute* for the Promotion of Mechanic Arts, p 3-6. Repeatedly, surmanes inscribed on the quilts are echoed in the Maryland Institute for the Promotion of the Mechanic's Art's male membership lists. The women's contribution to the fair is applauded in the opening and closing addresses. The quilts must have been prominent for the 1851 catalogue notes close to 170 quilts deposited for display.

Introduction

The Maryland Historical Society most recently showed its Baltimore Album Quilts in 2001. In the gallery, Victorian music played softly and the mood was reverential. For someone long on the Album journey this chance for a face-to-face visit was rare. This time certain characteristics struck me forcefully: the large format (16" and more) of many blocks; the frequency and high loft of padding in many simpler appliqués; and the rich, often woolen, embroidery in many blocks. I recalled how, in 1982, after first seeing "Baltimores" at the Baltimore Museum of Art, I'd chosen one classic Album's 12 ½" design size for the *Baltimore Beauties* series as functional for a contemporary quiltmaker's home. Hung in a museum, though, the large format quilts are impressive! At that earlier meeting, it was the one layer appliqués (the papercuts); the most ornate, realistically drafted blocks; and the Albums' stunning use of appliquéd shapes and fabric that I remembered most. Now, twenty years hence, exhilarating innovative Album appliqué techniques inspired by those old ones have been explored. This book's selection of out-of-print patterns invites you to revisit that journey and stitch that path yourself.

Because the Albums remain my first appliqué love, I'm always playing with possibilities. Thus the inspiration for the twelve new patterns—all pictured in the Color Section—are interpretations of classic Baltimore. Popular design motifs, personally interpreted, were integral to the old Baltimores. Different renderings of a motif may reflect joy in designing, desire to add one's "signature," an emphasis on icons, or simply an era with neither photocopiers nor discernable printed patterns. My own interpreting comes both from love of classic patterns and love of teaching appliqué techniques. The first four patterns, for example, are for cutaway appliqué, a simple, skill-honing method: It opened Baltimore's treasures to my hand and made me a dedicated appliquér. These four are new variations of the Wreathed Heart, the pattern I learned on, first published in *Spoken Without a Word*, 1983.

These open heart wreaths, when repeated up to eight times, can form a centered, equal-armed cross in a twenty-five block set (see page 114 in the Color Section.) This ingeniously unifying quilt set concept comes to us from antique Baltimore Albums. Hopefully these four hearts will spur on finished quilts! Moreover, cutaway blocks are among the most relaxing appliqué to do. Pattern 1 is appropriate even for a beginner's third block, if not her first, for it is an open practice field for points, curves, and inside corners. These wreathed heart variation blocks also invite advanced appliqué techniques: dimensional appliqué (Pattern 1); padded appliqué (Patterns 2, 3, and 4); and embroidered appliqué (Pattern 2). Patterns 5 through 9 invite padded appliqué and embroidery on a more complex level, and Patterns 10, 11, and 12 are ideal for revisiting the theorem appliqué techniques (stencil-shading with oil paintsticks or oil pastels) first taught in *Papercuts and Plenty*.

The Best of Baltimore Beauties, Part II is offered to serve the twenty-first century quiltmaker embarking upon the Album Quilt journey. It is a compendium of patterns from *Baltimore Album Quilts, Dimensional Appliqué, Baltimore Beauties and Beyond, Volume II, Papercuts and Plenty, Spoken Without a Word,* and a handful of my previously unpublished patterns. Each pattern is keyed to how-to lessons in *Baltimore Beauties and Beyond, Volume I.* Lesson by lesson, in informative increments, *Volume I* leads from the most basic one-layer appliqué to appliqué mastery. It demystifies the making of a complex classic quilt style, and *The Best of Baltimore* will serve *Volume I's* readers as an excellent source of further patterns. Other than *Volume I,* the *Baltimore Beauties* books (listed in About the Author on page 224) are out of print. Should you seek one, the most likely source is the auction site, E-bay, or elsewhere on the Internet.

This Book's Format

The Best of Baltimore Beauties, Part II patterns are grouped by the book in which they first appeared. Their numbers and graphic presentation are excerpted from their original books. You'll hear the tone of the pattern notes vary from book to book as I tried, for example, to convey historic background in *Baltimore Album Quilts* and focused on fabric manipulation in *Dimensional Appliqué*. Beyond being keyed to how-to lessons in *Volume I*, each pattern's historical context is set by the following designations:

Beyond Baltimore means beyond mid-nineteenth century Baltimore in time or place. These may be either old blocks in a style associated with Baltimore or contemporary blocks in Baltimore-style. If contemporary, the design is by the author or by a named contributor.

Classic Baltimore refers to a quilt or block pattern taken from a Baltimore Album Quilt of the mid-nineteenth century. A quilt is an authentic Baltimore Album Quilt if inscribed (or placed by provenance) with the geographic location Baltimore and a date between 1844 and 1856.

Baltimore-style means a quilt or block pattern that looks as though it might originate in a mid-nineteenth century Baltimore Album Quilt but whose provenance is uncertain. This term is also used for contemporary work recognizably related to the style of old Baltimore.

How to Take a Pattern from This Book

Baltimore Beauties and Beyond, Volume I (1989) originated a pattern transfer system whereby a 12 ½" pattern square could be presented at a set fraction of the whole pattern per book page. A 12 ½" (block size) square of freezer paper is folded into quadrants, shiny side inside, and the pattern is traced onto the paper's flat side, unit by unit. This "quadrant" pattern transfer method has now become the norm for quilt magazines and

books. The patterns are presented in one-eighth sections (two per pattern page), up to patterns presented in four quadrants on four pattern pages. For complete pattern transfer instruction, see "Pattern Transfer" in *Volume I*, pages 21–25. If you are familiar with that method, the following summary should suffice.

Patterns presented at ⅛ or ¼: Papercut (snowflake) patterns are presented first in each book excerpt. These are patterns cut from paper folded into eighths, much as school children scissors-cut snowflakes. Such patterns can be appliquéd from a single layer of cloth. In this sense they are the simplest patterns in Baltimore's Albums. But because, like snowflakes, the cut designs can be complex, some of them can also be a challenge to stitch! By separating one element, say the blossoms, from a papercut pattern, it can be appliquéd in two layers.

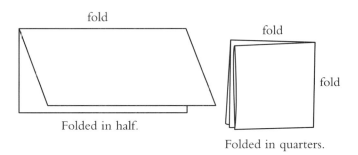

fold

Folded in half.

fold

fold

Folded in quarters.

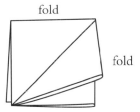

fold

fold

Folded in eighths front to front and back to back.

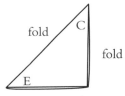

fold

fold

C

E

Folded in eighths and marked.

Hint: After folding the 12 ½" square of freezer paper into eighths, mark the center (where the folds meet) with a C for center. Mark the point where the hypotenuse meets the raw edges with an E for edge. Mark C and E on the top side of the folded paper. Then turn it over and mark the underside of the paper. When you open the paper, you can trace the pattern fraction onto either of the two wedges marked C/E, knowing that they will be on the outside when you refold and staple the paper prior to cutting its pattern. Use repositionable tape to hold the paper in place (matching Cs and Es) over the book as you trace.

Patterns presented at ½ of the block: two pattern pages. These patterns are first traced onto a 12 ½" square of freezer paper folded into quarters and marked C and E as above. The full block diagram shows you which half of the pattern is presented as quarter #1 and which as quarter #2. Trace the pattern onto the first folded freezer paper quadrant and then the second. Staple, then cut the pattern double on the fold.

Patterns presented at ¼ of the block: four pattern pages. These patterns are first traced onto a 12 ½" square of freezer paper folded into quarters. The full block diagram shows you which quarter to trace from which pattern page and numbers their tracing sequence.

Separate pattern elements: Basket patterns to be traced on the fold, then cut-out double, are stacked several to a page. Because baskets, urns, and vases invite you to customize their contents, these patterns are included for inspiration but without a full block drawing.

Supplementary Resources for *The Best of Baltimore Beauties II*

Baltimore Beauties and Beyond, Volume I remains the essential manual for learning Baltimore Album appliqué. For further details on basic appliqué in general, you'll appreciate *Appliqué 12 Easy Ways!*, winner of the Quilt Industry Classics Best Appliqué Book Award. Its sequel, *Fancy Appliqué: 12 Lessons to Enhance Your Skills* does just what its subtitle promises. All three of these technique books are published by C&T Publishing. Whether you are a beginner looking for additional blocks to stretch your skills or someone like me who just can't get enough of Album Appliqué, this book is for you. It comes with my heartfelt thanks and appreciation for your companionship on this uplifting journey.

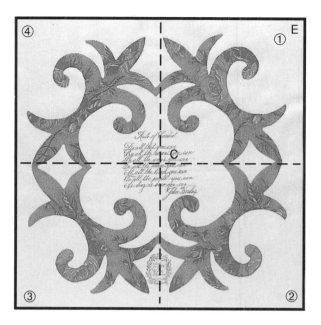

PATTERN #1: "Fleur-de-Lis Medallion I"

Type: Classic "Baltimore" (from quilt inscribed "1844" and "Baltimore.")

To make this block, refer to *Volume I*, Lessons 1 or 2.

The fleur-de-lis was so very popular a motif that it was often included as a secondary motif in other more complex patterns. This version, with four units forming a medallion center, must have taken a great stretch of the imagination to compose. But since its open center offered an attractive frame for an inscription, it too was repeated and was itself subject to creative adaptations.

Finely appliquéd by Gerri Rathbun, John Wesley's "Rule of Conduct" has been inscribed in this block's center: "Do all the good you can, By all the means you can, In all the ways you can, In all the places that you can, At all

continued on page 217

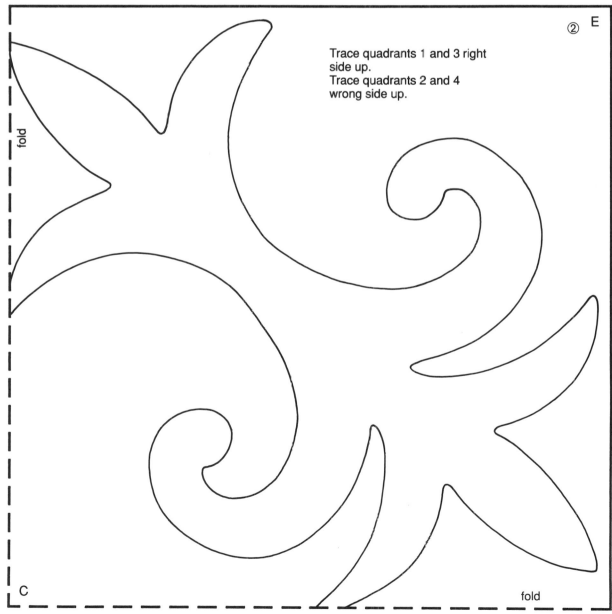

Trace quadrants 1 and 3 right side up.
Trace quadrants 2 and 4 wrong side up.

PATTERN #2: "Fleur-de-Lis II"*

Type: Baltimore-style

To make this block, refer to *Volume I*, Lesson 1 or 2.

Detail: *Volume I*, quilt #7.

The fleur-de-lis carries religious and political symbolism, standing for the Trinity and the Virgin Mary; as the emblem of "Light, Life, and Power," it is the national emblem of France. Might Baltimorean women, either those old enough to span the Revolutionary years, or younger ones kept close to the struggle against tyranny by the recent War of 1812, have wanted to memorialize the famed Frenchman Marquis de Lafayette in their quilts? For a fuller discussion of this, see Pattern #21.

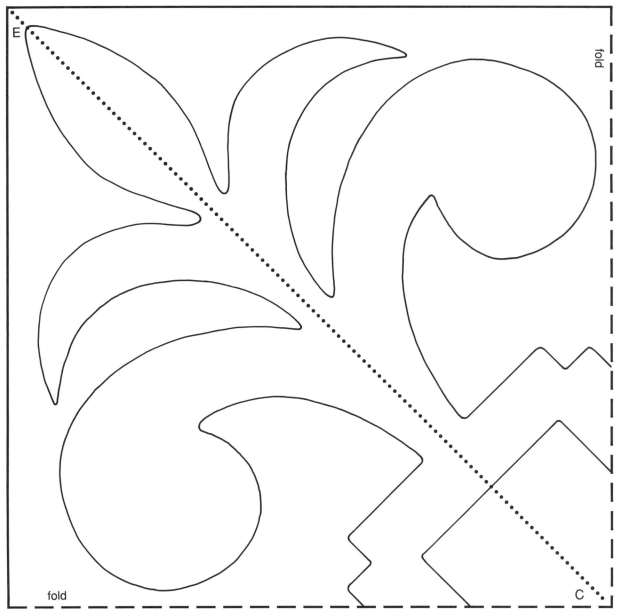

PATTERN #4: "Betty Alderman's Scherenschnitte"

Type: "Beyond"

To make this block, refer to *Volume I*, Lesson 1 or 2.

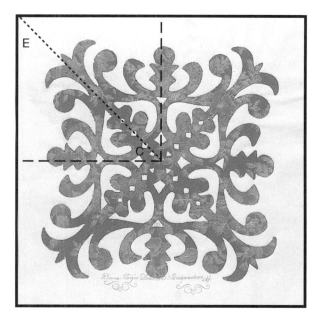

This graphic block is an original scherenschnitte ("scissor-cutting" in German) design by Betty Alderman. Betty was part of a magnificent Baltimore-style Album quiltmaking surprise gift for Laurene Sinema. Presented in appreciation by some associates, friends, and her 1988-89 Baltimore Album class, this was a true token of esteem. Laurene joins Mary Sue Hannan as the second person I know to receive such an accolade. (The quilt made for Mary Sue is shown in the Color Section in Volume I.) Like Mary Sue's quilt, Laurene's was presented as a completed top accompanied by a substantial fund to have it quilted professionally.

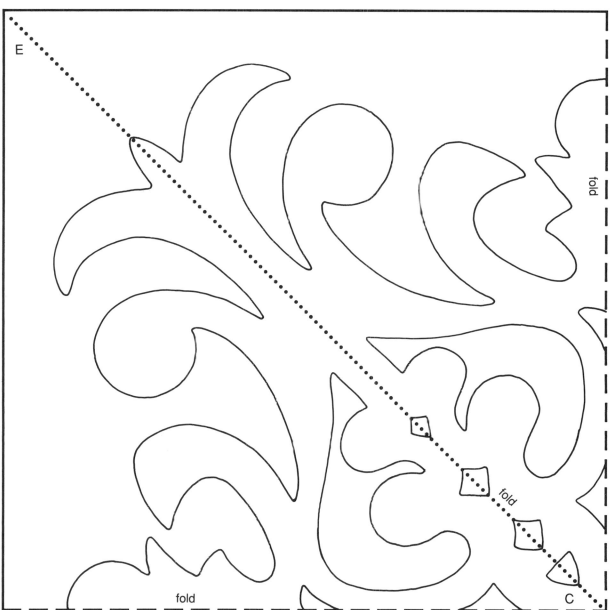

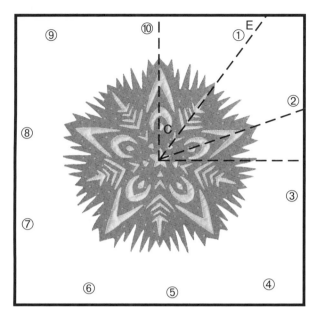

PATTERN #5: "Sylvia's *Wycinanki*"*

Type: "Beyond"

To make this block, refer to *Volume I*, Lesson 1 or 2.

German-influenced papercutting seems to have had a strong impact on the classic Baltimore Album Quilts. Papercutting in general has been a highly refined folk art in many cultures. Like some of the floral depictions and embellishments, it seems to reflect the influence of older folk art stylizations in these quilts. Here, Sylvia Pickell, in designing her 1985-86 quilt "Immigrant Influences: Album of Heritage" (*Volume I*, photo 31), wanted to show a typically Polish papercut design called *wycinanki*. She has captured the style well with its sharp spikey look. It is a tour de force of straight edges, perfect points, and masterpiece cutwork appliqué. This one pattern follows a completely different transfer sequence from the others, being based on tenfolds of the pattern square.

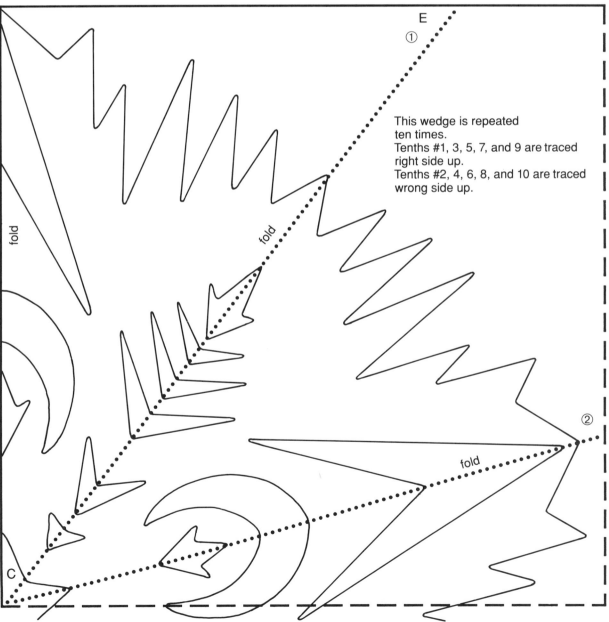

This wedge is repeated ten times.
Tenths #1, 3, 5, 7, and 9 are traced right side up.
Tenths #2, 4, 6, 8, and 10 are traced wrong side up.

PATTERN #6: "Hearts and Swans I and II"

Type: "Beyond"

To make this block, refer to *Volume I*, Lesson 1 or 2.

I was asked to teach appliqué at "Quilt Expo Europa 1990" in Odense, Denmark, the home of Hans Christian Andersen. This charming writer shared the same passion for papercuts as is reflected in the classic Album quilts. Determined to teach appliqué on a Hans Christian Andersen theme, I designed a number of blocks, including "Hearts and Swans." Because a circular red papercut makes an excellent classic Album Quilt center block, Mary Wise Miller made Version II, reduced to allow room for the inscription. Equally challenged, Georganna Clark made Version I.

continued on page 217

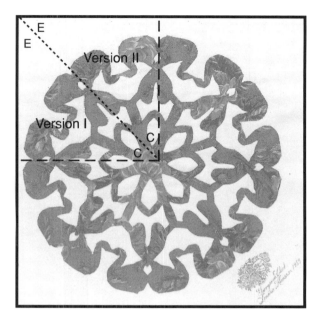

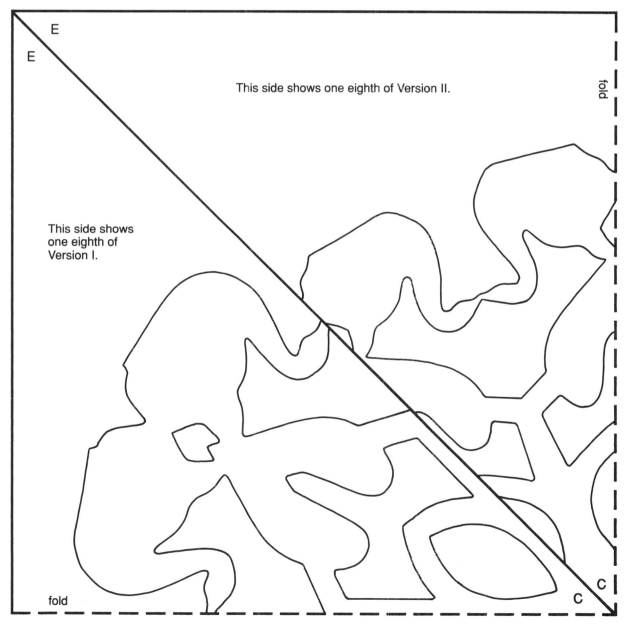

This side shows one eighth of Version II.

This side shows one eighth of Version I.

fold

fold

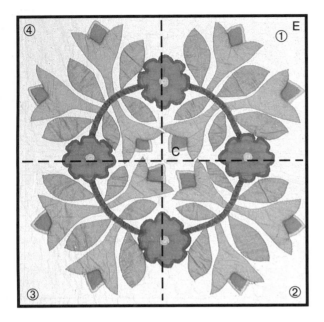

PATTERN #7: "Rose of Sharon II"

Type: Classic "Baltimore"

To make this block, refer to *Volume I*, Lessons 1 or 2, and 5 or 10.

Rose of Sharon I appears, unnumbered, in *Spoken Without a Word*; hence this is Version II. They are basically the same block, but this time the wreath has a lushly charming fullness to it. The pattern is drawn so it can be sewn as shown in separate unit applique or the green portions may be done by cutwork applique from one fabric. I have always called this the Rose of Sharon though Cuesta Benberry, who is very knowledgeable about such things, calls it a President's Wreath. Lore has it that after the Civil War, the Rose of Sharon blocks came to be known as President's Wreath.

PATTERN #8: "Folk Art Flower Wheel"

Type: Classic "Baltimore"

To make this block, refer to Volume I, Lesson 5.

These flowers around a cutwork wheel have a strong German, or "Pennsylvania Dutch" aspect. This particular stylization, with the inlaid flowers, simple shapes, and bold clear colors seems to be a design style which constitutes a minor and repeated theme in the classic Baltimore Album Quilts. Baltimore, during the three decades before the Civil War, was the port of entry for thousands of German immigrants. Though some earned passage for the return journey aboard Baltimore's cotton and tobacco exporting boats, many stayed. Because a strong Methodist connection to the Baltimore Albums is well documented, it is noteworthy that certain of Baltimore's Methodist churches were essentially German churches.

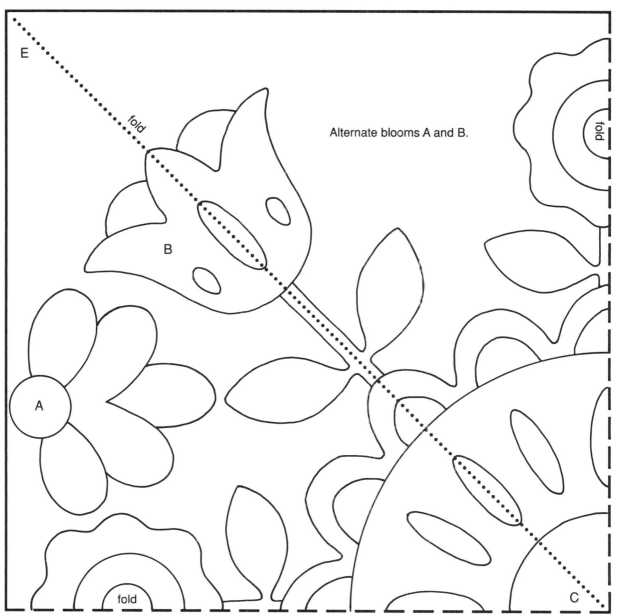

E

fold

Alternate blooms A and B.

fold

B

A

fold

C

PATTERN #10: "Red Vases and Red Flowers"

To make this block, refer to *Volume I*, Lesson 5.

Detail: Volume I, quilt #6. Design from Montgomery County, Maryland, inscribed in part, "Mary, Remember me/ William Thomas Johnson/1851." Original quilt in the collection of the DAR Museum, Washington, D.C.

What flower might this be? Dr. Dunton refers to a wreath of similar-looking flowers in the Samuel Williams quilt as passionflowers, replete with Christian symbolism. Botanical prints graced domestic interiors and botanical expeditions surely disembarked in this major port city. New specimens were quickly portrayed in her Albums: The Christmas cactus, moss rose (introduced to the U.S. in 1840), and ornamental peppers from Mexico. The Baltimore Era was also the heyday of Natural History!

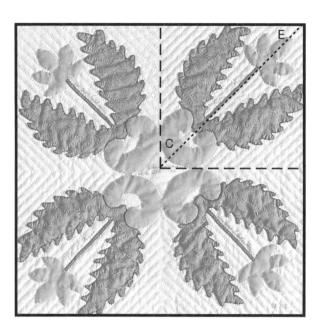

PATTERN #11: "Victorian Favorite"

Type: Classic "Baltimore"

To make this block, refer to *Volume I*, Lesson 5.

Detail: Volume I, quilt #6.

This pattern abounds in the classic appliqué Album Quilts. The block's center has a version of an almost Ionic motif that reads as a vase. In Freemasonry, which permeated the American decorative arts of the eighteenth to middle-nineteenth century, the Ionic order symbolizes Wisdom. In addition, acanthus leaves mean Admiring of the Fine Arts, also a Masonic virtue. The Album quiltmakers, seem so fond of symbolism, so sympathetic to the tenents of Freemasonry and Odd Fellowdom, that these influences must be seriously considered.

continued on page 217

PATTERN #14: "Fleur-de-Lis with Rosebuds IV"

Type: "Beyond"

To make this block, refer to *Volume I*, Lessons 1 or 2, and 6.

This is one of my original versions of the popular fleur-de-lis and rosebud block. Why design more when there are already so many? I sought another opened-center version to frame an inked portrait of people, a building, or a scene. In paper-cutting the possibilities, I found this particular one charming with its square-on-point center formed by buds and leaves inside the framing wreath stem.

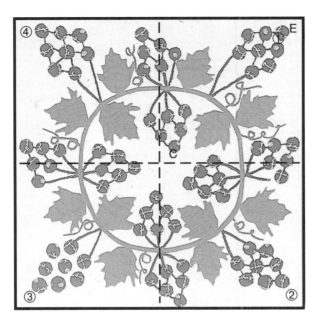

PATTERN #15: "Grapevine Wreath II"

Type: Baltimore-style

To make this block, refer to *Volume I*, Lessons 1 or 2, and 9.

This highly stylized grapevine intrigued me with its very realistic leaves and its Chinese-checker-like grapes. This precise grapebunch layout occurs elsewhere in these quilts, but infrequently. Excited, I imagined a seaman returning from the Orient, his gift to his Baltimore quiltmaking bride, a game of Chinese checkers. I was thus disappointed to find that Chinese checkers is a modern pastime, being a 1930s version of the game "Halma."

continued on page 217

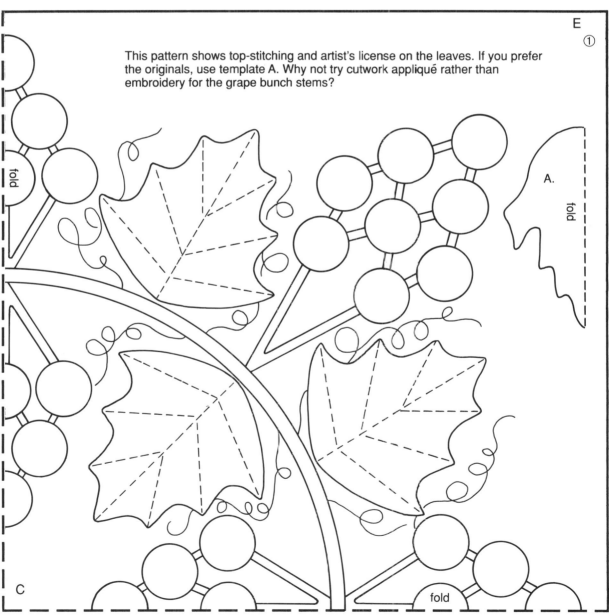

This pattern shows top-stitching and artist's license on the leaves. If you prefer the originals, use template A. Why not try cutwork appliqué rather than embroidery for the grape bunch stems?

PATTERN #16: "Strawberry Wreath II"

Type: Baltimore-style

To make this block, refer to *Volume I*, Lessons 5 and 9.

A classic-style Album Quilt block, this Strawberry Wreath is embellished with embroidery. Being circular, the wreath could intend Eternal Things and its strawberries Esteem and Love, or Intoxication and Delight. The strawberry leaves symbolize Completion and Perfection.

In the antique original, this block is heavily wool-embroidered with satin stitch around the strawberries and their hulls. The edges of the leaves are straight-stitched. The stems, too, are embroidered. Rows of stem or chain stitch are suggested for the stems.

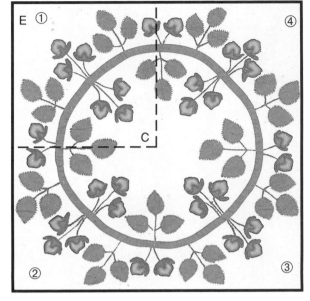

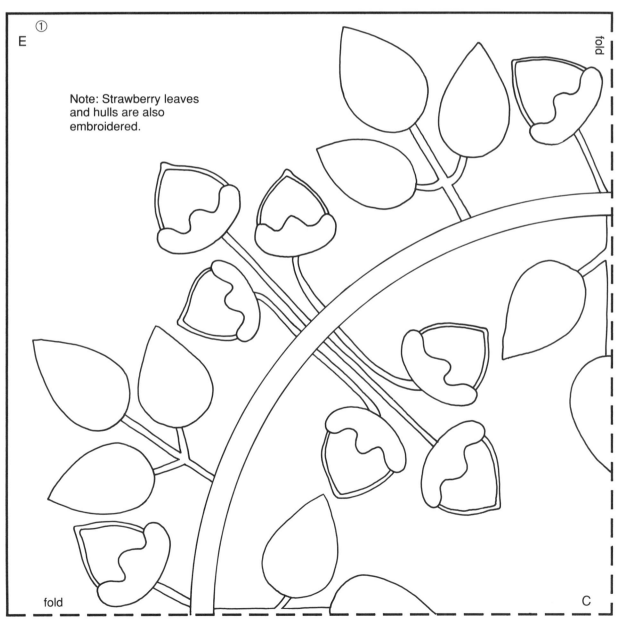

Note: Strawberry leaves and hulls are also embroidered.

PATTERN #18: "Circular Sprays of Flowers"

Type: Baltimore-style

To make this block, refer to *Volume I*, Lessons 1 or 2, 5 or 10.

This is a charming block and refreshingly easy to make! Perhaps there was a real competition going on, if only within a given quiltmaker's breast, to come up with as many conceivable ways to show sprays of flowers as possible: in baskets, vases, cornucopias; set in square, round, lyre, or heart-shaped wreaths, and in single sprays or double or tied as bouquets. This charming way of showing a wreath seems truly unique.

continued on page 217

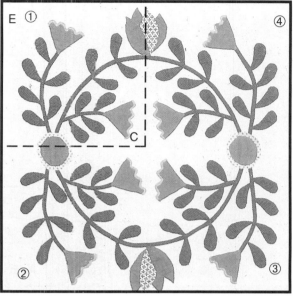

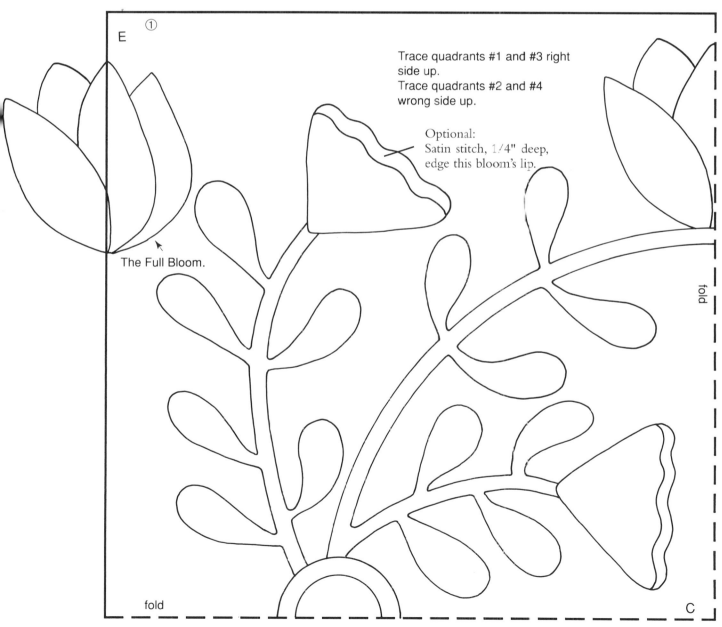

Trace quadrants #1 and #3 right side up.
Trace quadrants #2 and #4 wrong side up.

Optional:
Satin stitch, 1/4" deep, edge this bloom's lip.

The Full Bloom.

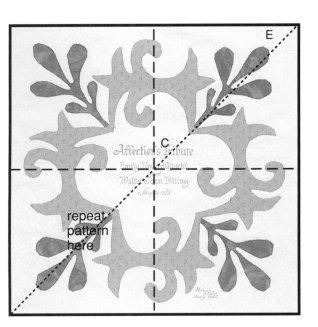

PATTERN #21: "Fleur-de-Lis Medallion II"

Type: Classic "Baltimore"

To make this block, refer to *Volume I*, Lessons 1 or 2, 5 or 10.

One specific reason for the popular inclusion of the fleur-de-lis could be what can be called none other than love for the gallant Marquis de Lafayette, a French hero of the American Revolution.

With wild enthusiasm, the American populace welcomed him back on his 1784 visit to the United States. The citizens of Maryland bestowed permanent citizenship upon him, making him one of their own.

PATTERN #21: "Fleur-de-Lis Medallion II"

Second Page

In the spring of 1781, the "dashing young Marquis de Lafayette" had ridden into Baltimore, leading his troops "on the way South and stopped for the night. The good women of the town organized a ball in his honor."

An elder statesman, his triumphal farewell tour of America in 1824 brought untrammeled adulation as a man, a hero, and a symbol of the American Revolution. Certainly a symbol of French Republicanism, the fleur-de-lis (particularly when embellished, as here, with laurel) may well have memorialized Lafayette.

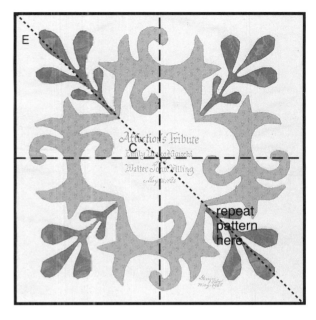

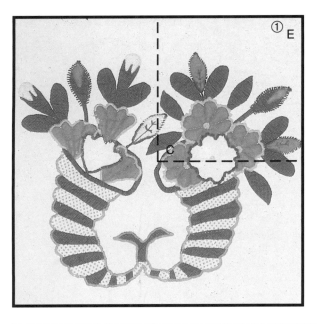

PATTERN #24: "Rose Cornucopias"

Type: Baltimore-style

To make this block, refer to *Volume I*, Lessons 5, 9, or 10.

If you covet cornucopias for your quilt, this is our simplest rendition yet, though to keep it in the moderately easy category, one would have to side-step the exquisite, but time-consuming embroidery. Note that in the original, pursuing what seems to have been a Victorian aesthetic ideal of asymmetry, each horn holds differently rendered blooms. A cornucopia speaks of Abundance, rose of Love. Were I a betting woman, I'd say our block's subject is love, sweet love, and plenty of it!

Cornucopias were a popular Victorian decorative motif, bespeaking the earth's plenty.

PATTERN #24: "Rose Cornucopias"

Second Page

Edna Barth tells us in *Turkeys, Pilgrims, and Indian Corn* that the cornucopia motif goes back at least to classical Greece. "The Greeks had several myths about cornucopia, their name for the horn of plenty. One of these tells of Amalthea, a goat who suckled the infant god Zeus. Once Amalthea broke off one of her horns. Filling it with fruits and flowers, she gave it to Zeus. To show his gratitude, Zeus later set the goat's image in the sky as the constellation Capricorn." In another myth, Amalthea was a nymph who raised Zeus on goat's milk. The grateful young god broke off the goat's horn and gave it to his kind foster mother. This horn of plenty would supply her an abundance of whatever she wanted. Clearly gratitude for abundance is also symbolized by the cornucopia motif from ancient harvest festivals to our own Thanksgiving.

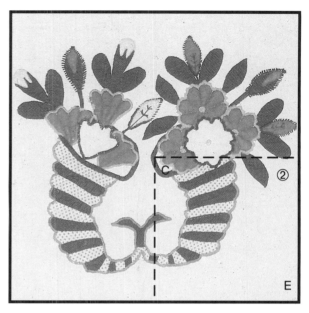

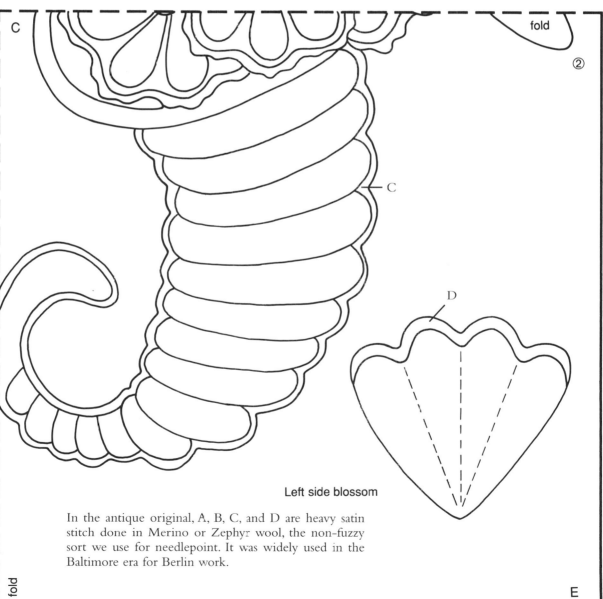

Left side blossom

In the antique original, A, B, C, and D are heavy satin stitch done in Merino or Zephyr wool, the non-fuzzy sort we use for needlepoint. It was widely used in the Baltimore era for Berlin work.

PATTERN #30: "Vase with Fruits and Flowers"

Type: Classic "Baltimore"

To make this block, refer to *Volume I*, Lessons 5, 9, or 10.

Wild and wonderful, this block seems filled with symbolism, but the secret's not out yet. With careful precision, the clusters of four circles—two red, two yellow—proceed around the bouquet, and lest you wonder if they be another fruit, the cherries dangle on long stems. The cherries mean Sweet Character, Good Deeds. If "cherry twins," they mean Love's Charms and are a good luck symbol.

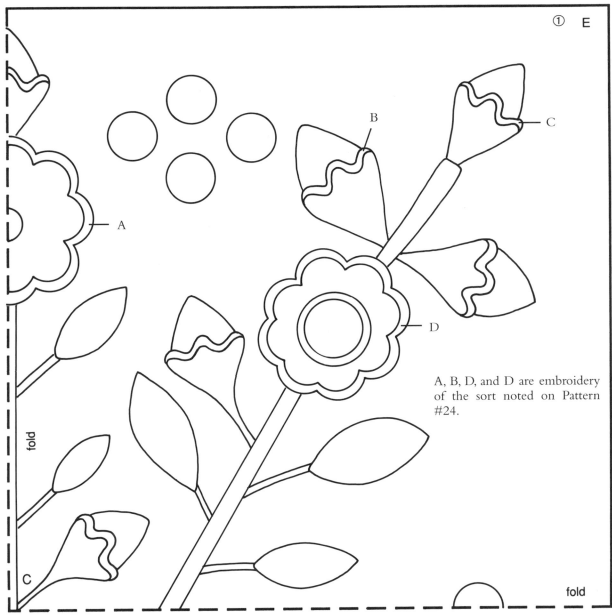

A, B, D, and D are embroidery of the sort noted on Pattern #24.

PATTERN #30: "Vase with Fruits and Flowers"

Second Page

Roses mean Love, that much is known. If you decode this pretty presentation of posies, please pass the poem along! For efficiency, we have shown this as a two-page pattern, where its asymmetry would otherwise require four. All the elements are here, however, and by mixing leaves and buds a bit, you can capture the original again.

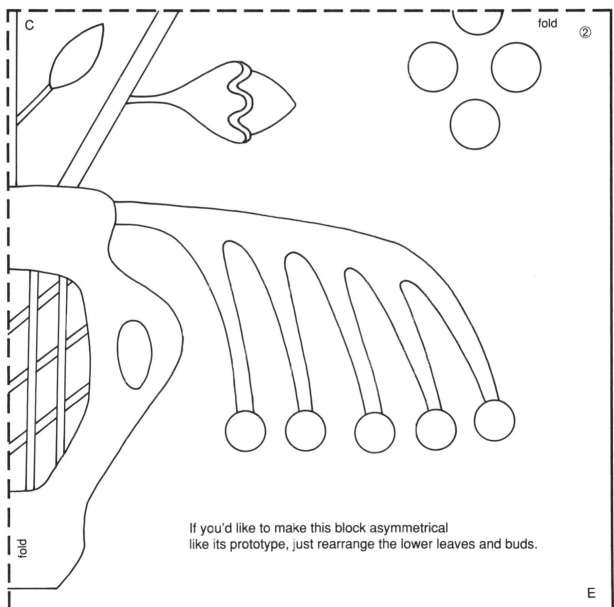

If you'd like to make this block asymmetrical like its prototype, just rearrange the lower leaves and buds.

PATTERN #41: "Victorian Basket of Flowers IV"

Type: Classic "Baltimore"

To make this block, refer to *Volume I*, Lessons 5, 9, or 10.

Detail: Volume I, quilt #2.

Ornate, realistic, Victorian, a woven basket—and yet not overwhelming at that. This basket, with a bit of ruffled trim at the bottom, is a style repeated in an exquisite Album Quilt belonging to the Smithsonian Institution in Washington.

PATTERN #41: "Victorian Basket of Flowers IV"

Second Page

The upturned base framed by a scallop, as though by eyelashes, is found frequently in the antique Baltimores. Might it represent the "All-Seeing Eye of God"? This symbol was so important, so widely understood in our country's early centuries, that to this day it is atop the pyramid on our dollar bill.

PATTERN #41: "Victorian Basket of Flowers IV"

Third page

PATTERN #41: "Victorian Basket of Flowers IV"

Fourth Page

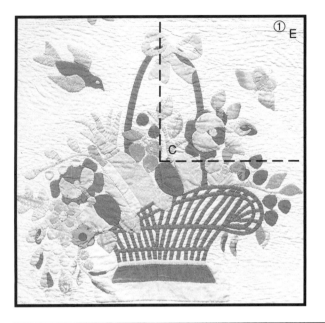

PATTERN #42: "Victorian Basket V with Fruits and Flowers"

Type: Classic "Baltimore"

To make this block, refer to *Volume I*, Lesson 5, 7, 9, or 10.

This particularly graceful basket shape is usually filled with flowers. In an artful play on that theme, this one includes fruit as well. The elegant touch of what may be a pearl-handled fruit knife usually accompanies a cut watermelon. Here it is seen with a fresh pineapple, symbol of Hospitality and imbued with the message "You are perfect!" Bird, butterfly, basket, and contents are probably replete with symbolic intent, but that is left for you to decipher!

PATTERN #42: "Victorian Basket V with Fruits and Flowers"

Second Page

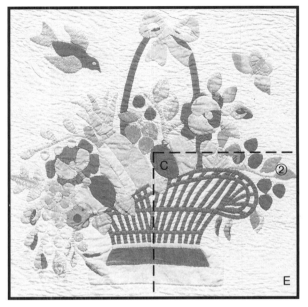

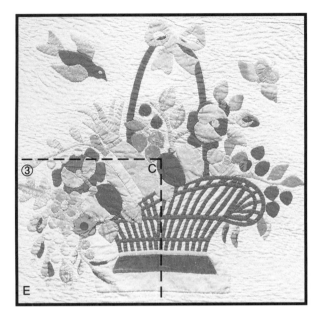

PATTERN #42: "Victorian Basket V with Fruits and Flowers"

Third Page

PATTERN #42: "Victorian Basket V with Fruits and Flowers"

Fourth Page

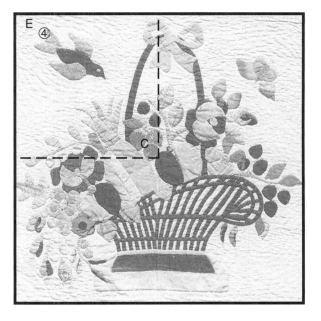

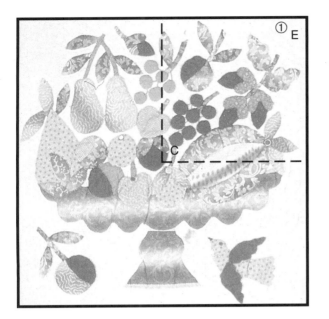

PATTERN #44: "Scalloped Epergne of Fruit"

Type: Classic "Baltimore"

To make this block, refer to *Volume I*, Lesson 5, 9, or 10.

Our block presents a highly stylized version of the fruit in a raised glass stand motif. Epergnes—pedestaled, ornamental serving dishes— were a popular decorative glassware at the time of this quilt's making. In elegant variety, epergnes were depicted in some detail in these Album Quilts. My observation, by no means definitive, is that this scalloped version comes early on the chart of these quilts as in this 1846-47 quilt. By contrast, some, possibly later, epergnes are depicted in finer detail, often with cut glass ornamentation on the bowl.

PATTERN #44: "Scalloped Epergne of Fruit"

Second Page

Some rather sophisticated fabric adds to the elegance of this block. Dr. Dunton describes it in his usual exact manner: "The watermelon is of a shaded and figured green with meat of a figured pink stripe and inked seeds. Two other figured prints form the fruit. The pineapple is the…yellow [print with very small black dots and larger dots encircled with small dots] with the same figured green as the watermelon. This is also used for the foliage of the upper fruits and of the fruit in the lower left corner, the right half being red. The upper bunch of grapes is blue, the lower red. The three strawberries to the right are red, their seeds indicated with white stitching. Their hulls are a figured green…. The pears on the upper left are of a moiré green shaded to white" (*Old Quilts*, p. 22).

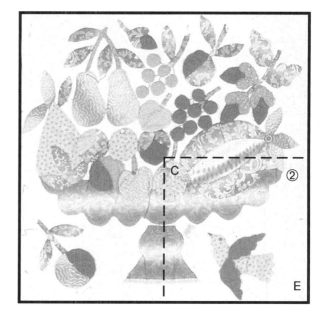

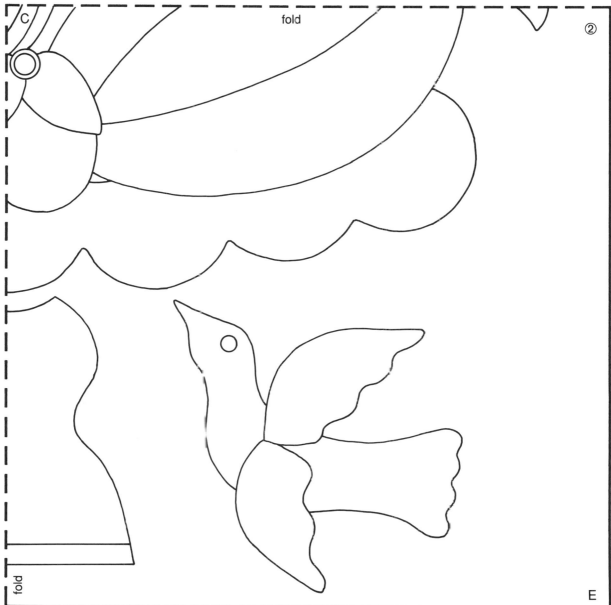

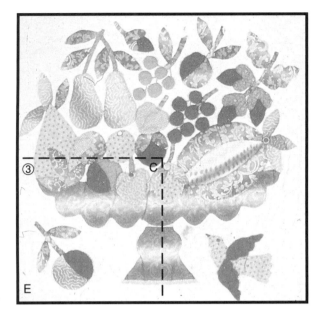

PATTERN #44: "Scalloped Epergne of Fruit"

Third Page

PATTERN #44: "Scalloped Epergne of Fruit"

Fourth Page

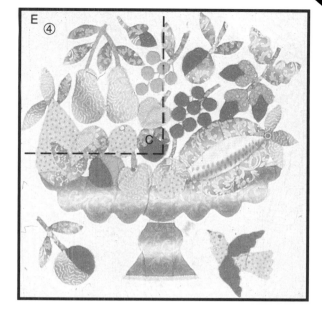

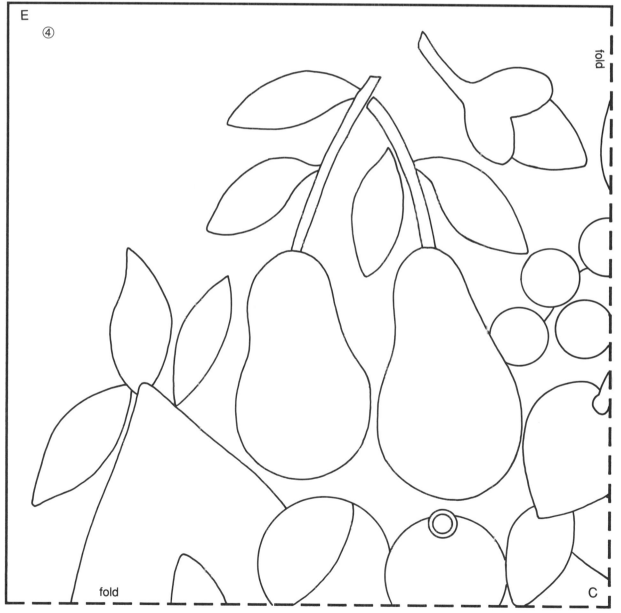

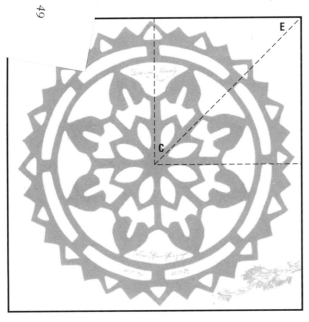

PATTERN #1: "Hans Christian Andersen's Danish Hearts"

Type: "Beyond" Baltimore

To make this block, refer to *Volume I*, Lesson 1, 2, or 11.

"Godfather could tell stories, cut pictures, and draw," wrote Hans Christian Andersen, seemingly of himself. This circle of hearts is a close facsimile of one of Hans Christian Andersen's nineteenth-century paper-cuts, now exquisitely appliqued by Eleanor Kay Green Hunzinger of Phoenix, Arizona. Elly Sienkiewicz drafted the pattern (and added the triangle edging) for a course in "Andersen and Applique," taught at Quilt Expo Europa 1990 in Andersen's birthplace, Odense, Denmark. A framed applique by Elly of an Andersen scherenschnitte was presented to the Mayor of Odense, for the Museum, by Karey Bresnahan, Director of Quilt Expo.

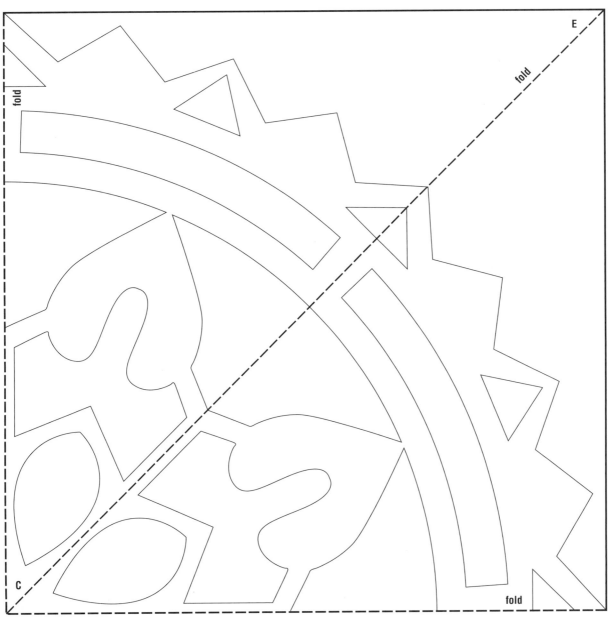

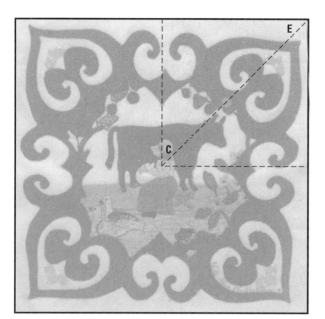

PATTERN #7: "Heart Medallion Frame"

Type: "Beyond" Baltimore

To make this block, refer to *Volume I*, Lesson 1, 2, or 11.

I designed this and the Acorn and Oak Leaf Frame as picture-block frames which would work well with the classic red scherenschnitte frame seen on the hunting Scene pattern in *Spoken Without a Word*. Small yellow candy-kiss shapes accent the corners. In the block, Katya and Her Cats, however, I forgot to include them. See *Volume I*, quilt #6, for a color picture of these blocks and to see how several framed blocks can help create an interior design in the quilt's set.

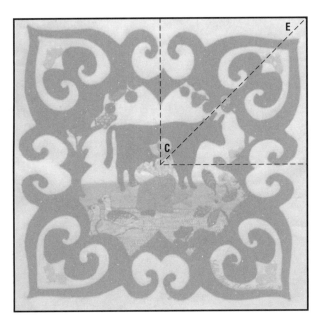

PATTERN #7: "Heart Medallion Frame"

Second Page

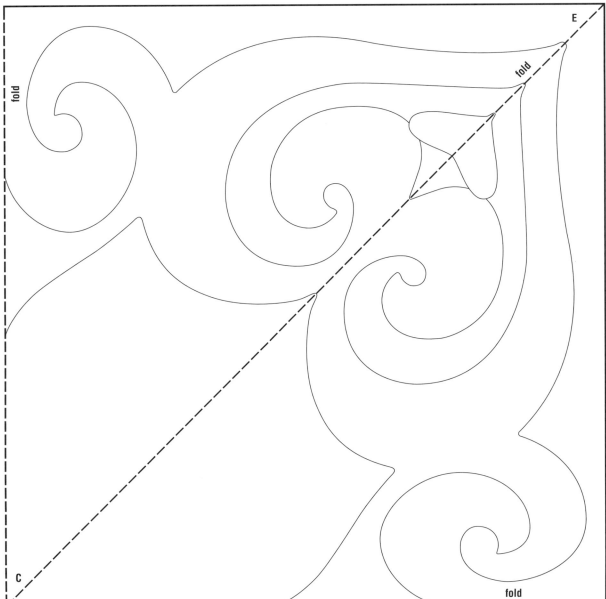

PATTERN #8: "Goose Girl Milking"

Type: "Beyond" Baltimore

To make this block, refer to *Volume I*, Lesson 5 or 10.

This scene fits the previous pattern, Heart Medallion Frame, and was inspired by a classic Album scene. One wonders what subject, what thought, encouraged these infrequent yet recurring bucolic scenes of a young lady with furred and feathered friends. Beautifully appliquéd here by Sally Glaze, the Heart Medallion Frame takes on a different look in an overall feathered red print.

For another view of this same bonneted maiden with geese see page 62. The pattern notes have more information about her. See also Pattern #17 from *Baltimore Beauties and Beyond*.

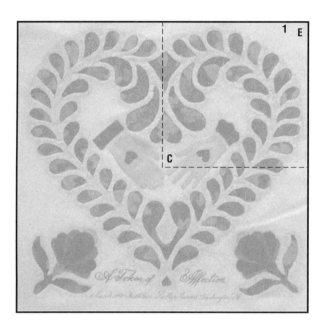

PATTERN #9: "Hearts and Hands in a Feather Wreath"

Type: "Beyond" Baltimore

To make this block, refer to *Volume I*, Lesson 1, 2, 3, or 10.

This is a third version of the feather-wreathed hearts that I designed for *Volume I*. It was never made because of the increasing difficulty in finding high-quality off-white background fabric which does not fray too badly for reverse applique. Kathy Mannix, my friend and neighbor, suggested that one of the printed white-on-white muslins might work well and proceeded to make this lovely block. She reports that it turned like butter and that the applique, petal by petal, is like eating candy—hard to stop!

continued on page 217

PATTERN #9: "Hearts and Hands in a Feather Wreath"*

(Second page)

Pattern Bridges

C   2

A Token of Affection

E

C   fold   2

fold

E

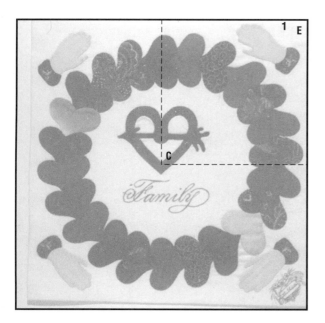

PATTERN #12: "Wreath of Hearts I (and II)"

Type: "Beyond" Baltimore Wreath of Hearts I is classic Baltimore and appears as a simple circle of hearts in the circa 1850 Album Quilt pictured in the *Quilt Engagement Calendar Treasury* (p. 148).

To make this block, refer to *Volume I*, Lesson 10.

While version II is "beyond" Baltimore, being of my own design, it looks quite Victorian and Baltimorean in Lisa Schiller's fine applique and fabrics. In part this vintage look comes from the heart, the hand, and the arrow – all Odd Fellow symbols which recur in the vintage Albums. Fraternal orders used symbols to teach precepts. Thus the arrow teaches the Odd Fellow "to make all efforts to save a brother when he is in peril; …the heart and hand urge the Odd Fellow to acts of mercy and benevolence;

continued on page 217

PATTERN #12: "Wreath of Hearts I (and II)"

Second Page

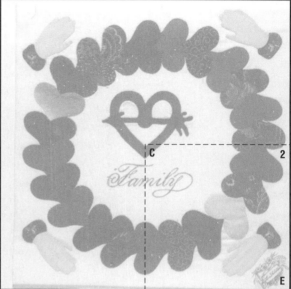

Heart Template

PATTERN #12: "Wreath of Hearts I (and II)"

Second Page

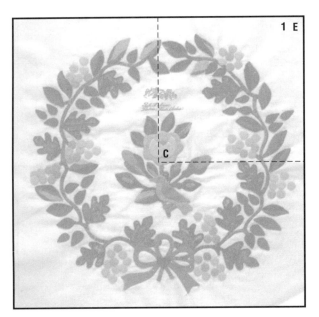

PATTERN #13: "Bird in a Fruit Wreath"

Type: Classic Baltimore

To make this block, refer to *Volume I*, Lesson 10.

Take up birdwatching in the classic Baltimore Albums and you will be richly rewarded. Though made in a temperate clime, those "natural history albums" are filled with tropical birds, exotic newly met species brought back under sail or steam from Africa and South America to be engraved in illustrated folios. There are, in these quilts, toucans, small African parrots ("love birds"), peacocks, and birds better known in that Audubon/Album Quilt era than now. But there are also doves, hummingbirds, thistle-finches ("distlefinks"), and eagles. I am quite sure that in the original block this was meant to be some very specific real bird, perhaps a sparrow, here beautifully wrought anew by Ruth Meyers.

PATTERN #13: "Bird in a Fruit Wreath"

Second Page

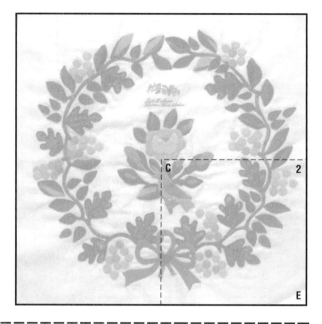

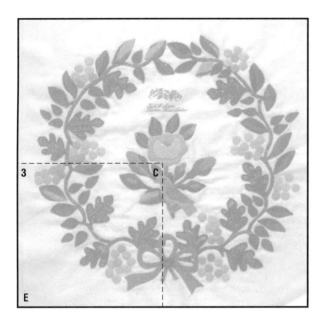

PATTERN #13: "Bird in a Fruit Wreath"

Third Page

PATTERN #13: "Bird in a Fruit Wreath"

Fourth Page

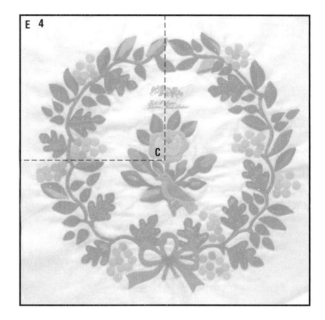

PATTERN #15: "Goose Girl"

Type: Baltimore-style

To make this block, refer to *Volume I*, Lesson 10.

As a classic quilt block, this scene comes in several versions. One wonders what the important elements in it are and whether it has some symbolic significance. For example, one Numsen family house/garden scene, shows this same Georgian house, the fence, the trees, the birds, but instead of the girl walking, there is an empty path with an ornate and bustling silk beehive at its end.

The *Oddfellows Monitor and Guide*, which illustrates and defines the nineteenth century American order's symbols, gives the beehive as a significant Rebekah symbol standing for the power of cooperative action.

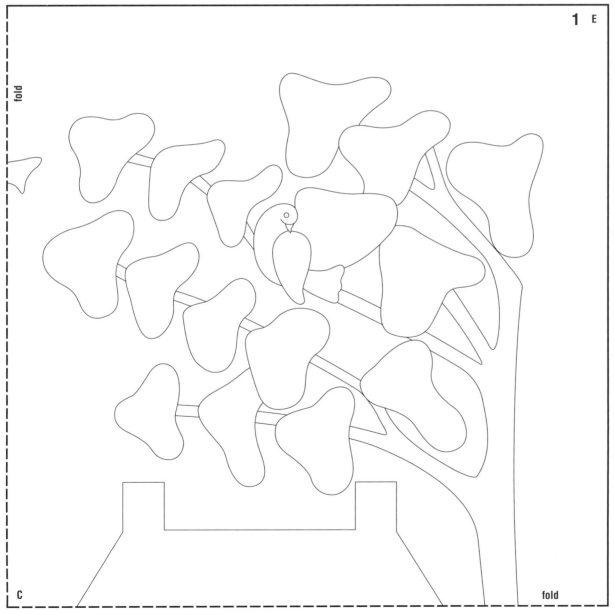

PATTERN #15: "Goose Girl"

Second Page

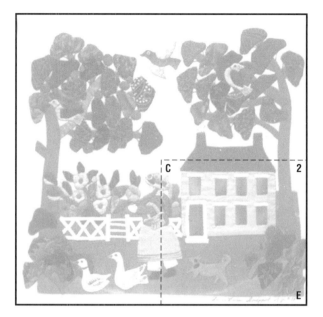

I hypothesize that this Pattern #15 scene (which is not unique) and the Numsen family scene depict a Rebekah (a wife of an Oddfellow) shown with a dog for fidelity, flock and flowers for domesticity, en route from her home to attend her Rebekah meeting. This hypothesis comes from my sense of these quilts after so many years of study, but also the fact that the Rebekah connection is substantiated by dates written on Baltimore Album Quilts. If one graphs the dates written on Album Quilts (published in museum catalogues from 1980 to present), the bell curve peaks at 1851–52, bracketing the year the Rebekkah Lodge first opened on Fels Point in Baltimore. Could the making of the blocks be connected with the teaching of Oddfellowdom's moral precepts for wives and daughters of Oddfellows –

PATTERN #15: "Goose Girl"

Third Page

or to fundraising for the building of the new auxiliary order's lodge? It is interesting in the former connection that older quilt lore called the Baltimore Album Quilts "Baltimore Brides quilts."

Another artifact connects this same Pattern #15 maiden to the Oddfellows: It is an engraving owned by the Winterthur Museum of Wilmington, Delaware. There the woman stands inside a draftsman's compass, itself circumscribed by a circle around which is written "Keep within compass and you will be sure to avoid many troubles which others endure." The compass is a major symbol of both the Freemasons and the Oddfellows, but it is the Oddfellows who are alone among all the extant fraternal orders in being the first order to admit women during the Baltimore Album Quilt era.

PATTERN #15: "Goose Girl"

Fourth Page

Whatever one concludes as to this block's origin and intent, Donna Collin's stitched version seems even more beautiful than any of its classic predecessors.

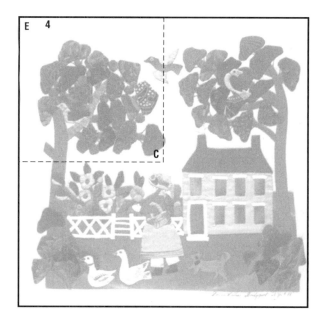

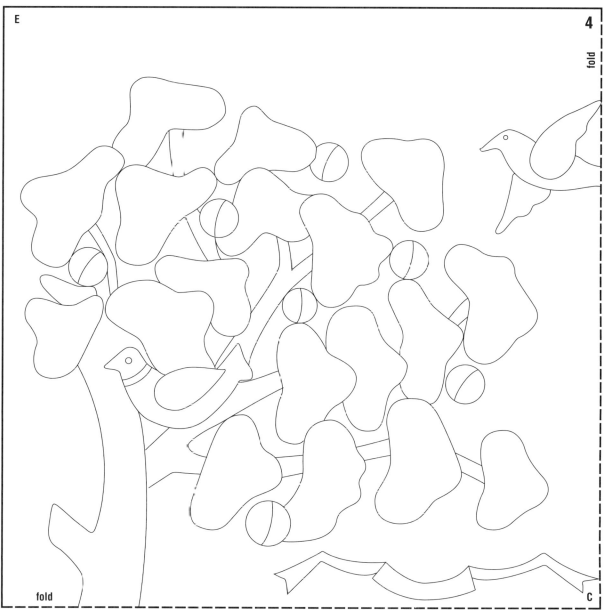

PATTERN #16: "Waterfowling"

Type: Baltimore-style

To make this block, refer to *Volume I*, Lesson 5 or 10.

Though relatively rare, picture blocks of men waterfowling are repeated in the classic quilts. Another version, shown to the left, illustrates the layout of our pattern but offers yet another classic interpretation of our theme. The square includes someone boating while the pattern taken from another quilt has a boat at anchor. The human characters vary in these hunting scenes, but fowl are always plentiful and a bird dog or two is always along. Dogs symbolize Fidelity and occur elsewhere in these quilts, as well. To this day, duck blinds dot Maryland waterways and fowling is still enjoyed. But in the Victorian Album Quilt

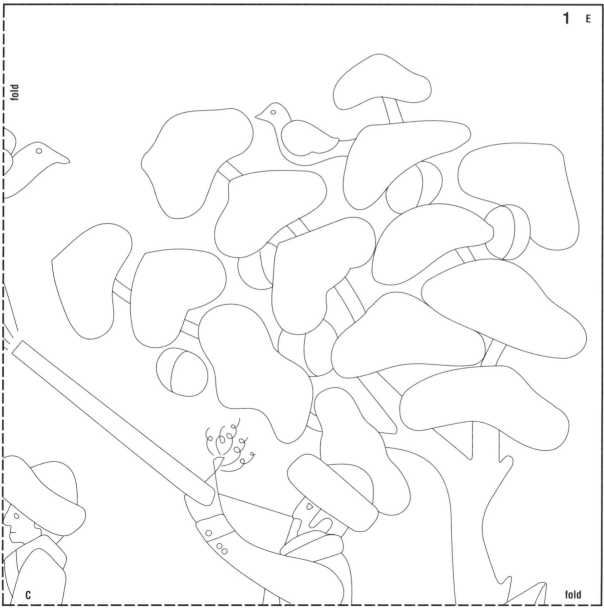

PATTERN #16: "Waterfowling"

Second Page

era, men hunting might also be seen as studying natural history and thus pursuing an edifying rational pleasure. The sport was useful in that it provided fresh victuals, but it also contained elements of instruction and moral uplift in that it took one into the great outdoors to marvel at God's plan.

PATTERN #16: "Waterfowling"

Third Page

PATTERN #16: "Waterfowling"

Fourth Page

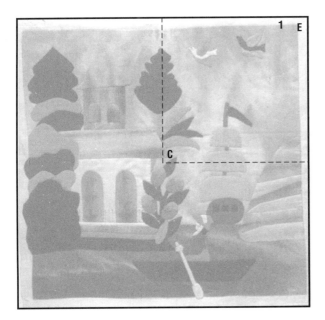

PATTERN #17: "Tropical Boating"

Type: Baltimore-style

To make this block, refer to *Volume I*, Lesson 5 or 10.

Reminiscent of a classic quilt block, this unique scene from an antique quilt seems greened by tropical foliage and quite exotic. A pagoda-like building and anchored clipper ship in the background bespeak far-off places. Yet the woman boating before us could be Baltimorean, perhaps a Victorian missionary's wife?

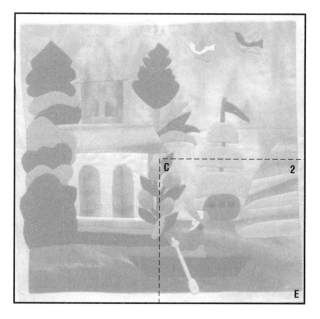

PATTERN #17: "Tropical Boating"

Second Page

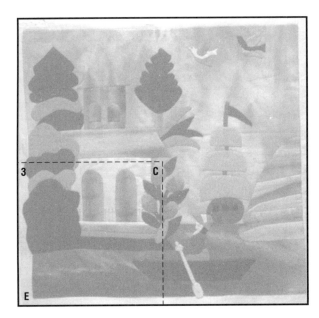

PATTERN #17: "Tropical Boating"

Third Page

PATTERN #17: "Tropical Boating"

Fourth Page

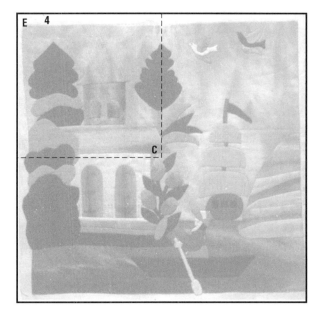

PATTERN #21: "The Peony Border"

Type: Classic Baltimore

To make this block, refer to *Volume I*, Lesson 1-3

The favorite classic borders could be described as center-running borders and edging borders. In center-running borders, a contiguous motif is continuously repeated along the border's center length (as in a vine or in a swag border wit connecting bow or flower). Edging borders decorate the border's outside edges with a contiguously repeated shape: scallops, a row of dogtooth triangles, steps and so forth. The exciting thing about center-running borders and edging borders is that they are splendidly "mix-and-Matchable." Where one quilt will have a simple dogtooth border edging with white space (dimensioned with quilting) in between, another will have a rose vine meandering between the serrate rows of edging.

Yet another will have the same vine, but with no appliquéd edging. This Peony Border is an edging border. The appliqué was originally a solid color, but this sort of cut-away motif looks great in a large print.

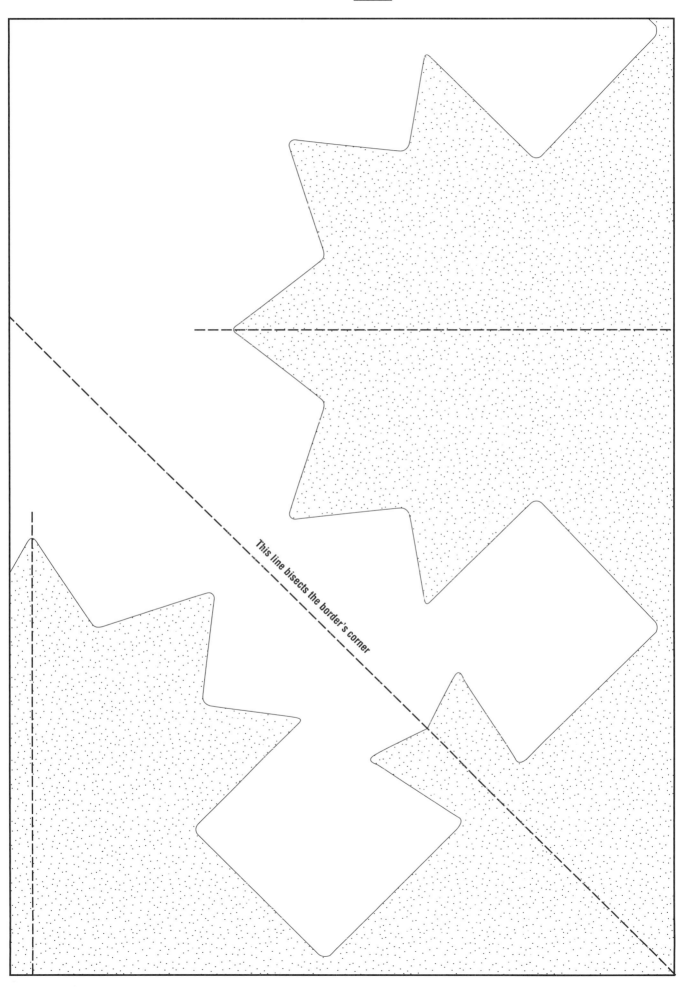

This line bisects the border's corner

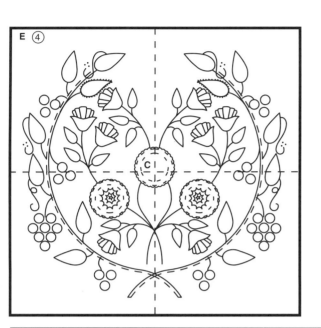

PATTERN #7: "Rick Rack Roses"

Type: "Beyond"; Designed by Gwendolyn LeLacheur

To make this block, refer to *Volume I*, Lessons 2 and 9. This charming block combines several dimensional flowers. It is fancy needlework approached in an easy straightforward way. Lovely to look at and fun to make! Gwen outlines her approach to this block:

1. Superfine Stems: Draw outer line only on fabric.
2. Leaves appliquéd, then outlined in buttonhole stitch (two strands of embroidery floss).
3. Grapes: Freezer paper (or 1/2" office dot) template underneath.
4. Rick Rack Flowers: 1 ¼ yards of jumbo rick rack one length twisted to interlock with the other.
5. Pleated Flowers: (instructions in Lesson 8).
6. Stems and French Knots: Embroider using two strands of embroidery floss.

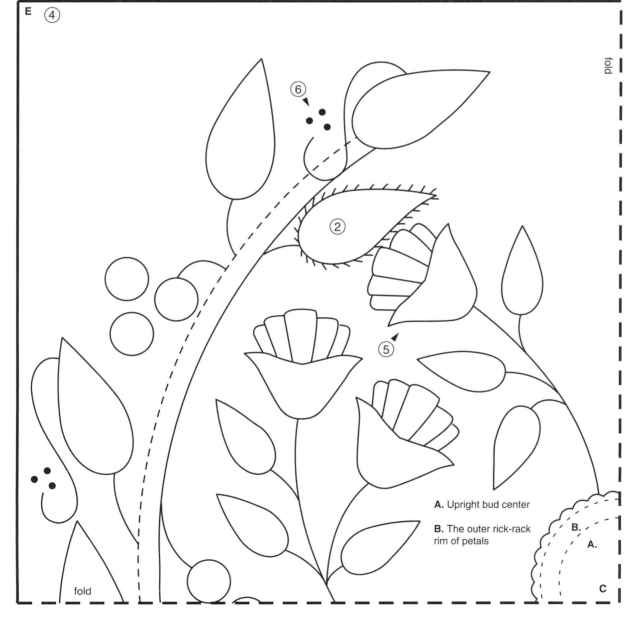

A. Upright bud center

B. The outer rick-rack rim of petals

PATTERN #7: "Rick Rack Roses"

Second page

Pleated Flowers:
1. Cut a 1" x 2 1/2" rectangle of cotton cloth. Iron under a 3/16" hem on the top and sides (see illustration A). To hold the hem, and then to hold the pleats, use a bit of liquid starch dabbed from the wrong side onto the seam. Or, suggests Gwen, use a strand of ThreadFuse™ laid inside each fold and pressed to bond it.
2. Accordion-pleat the hemmed rectangle into four pleats. Iron each pleat to press the creases in.
3. Tuck the bottom of the pleated rectangle into the flower's open calyx (see illustration B). Fan the pleats out a bit at the top of the bloom and appliqué in place.

Rick Rack Roses on page 218

Rick-Rack Roses:
Trace only dotted line onto fabric.

2 ½"

1"

A. Fold hem under on dotted line.

B. GwenLeLacheur's
Small Pleated Bloom

PATTERN #8: "Flower-Wreathed Heart II"

Type: "Baltimore-style"

To make this block, refer to *Volume I*, Lessons 1, 2, and 5.

Early in the Baltimore Album Revival, this block began to be made. I had put a similar pattern in *Spoken Without a Word*, and it was one of the first of the ornate Victorian blocks to be reproduced by modern needlewomen. But few reproduced it exactly.

PATTERN #8: "Flower-Wreathed Heart II"

Second Page

The combination of the heart shape, so comfortably well-known to us, and the flowers we love to fashion, seemed to encourage people to make this sweet pattern very much their own. The pattern given here differs a bit from that in *Spoken Without a Word*. It offers several additional flowers to be included in your version. They come with the invitation to twine this bouquet just as it pleases you.

Alternate Leaf and Blossoms.

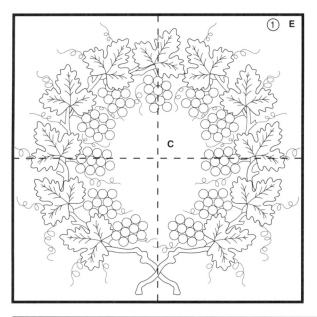

PATTERN #9: "Lovely Lane's Grapevine Wreath"

Type: classic "Baltimore"

To make this block, refer to *Volume I*, Lesson 9.

This block's antique original is a perfectly lovely piece of needle art. The leaves appear to be grape leaves cut from a print, then closely blanket or buttonhole stitched down, broderie perse style. The small stuffed grapes are shaded, their increasing intensities of hue giving a life-like depth to the clusters. The vine is not a simple stem, but seems also to have been cut from a print and embroidered down.

The leaf veins appear to have been printed or inked. The tendrils are chain stitched in one strand floss.

Flop pattern over to mark opposite side of wreath except top center bunch of grapes and leaf.

PATTERN #9: "Lovely Lane's Grapevine Wreath"

Second page

Tendrils in stitchery complete this block. Recognized long ago for its great beauty, this square became a classic quilt's center block. One wonders if the whole applique (stem, leaves, fruit) were not perhaps cut from one piece of cloth and reconstructed on the Album block. For whatever reason, the original appears to be one block of a kind among the antique Albums, but it is already beginning to be repeated by us in our Revival Albums.

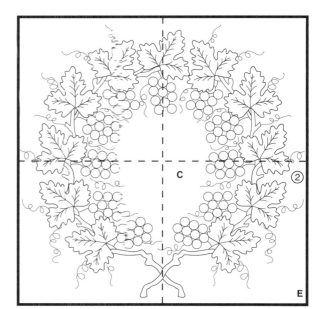

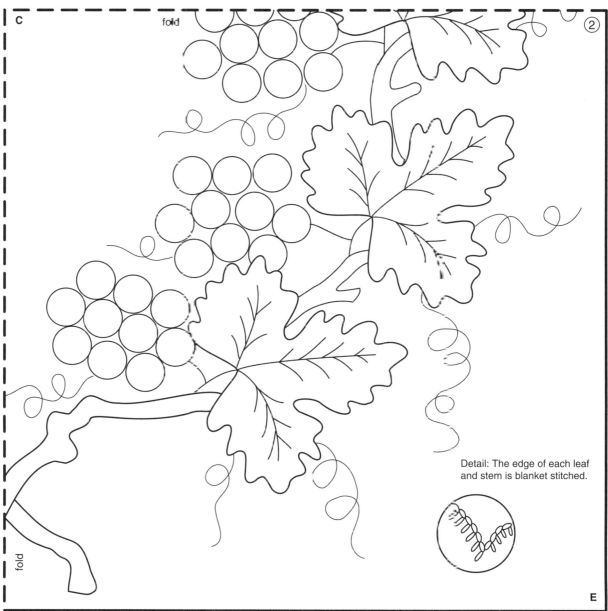

Detail: The edge of each leaf and stem is blanket stitched.

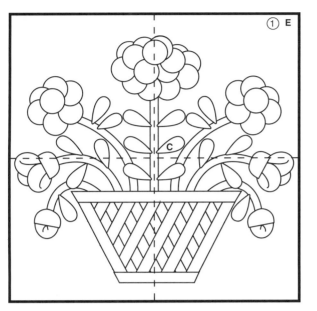

PATTERN #11: "Basket of Quarter Roses and Buds"

Type: "Beyond"; Designed by Melody Bollay

To make this block, refer to *Volume I*, Lessons 5, 9, and 10.

A few years ago, a set of unfinished Album blocks was discovered, preserved in a drawer long warped shut in the Sands House, the oldest surviving wooden house in Annapolis, Maryland. Among the blocks was a basted bouquet with pleated flowers and a rose constructed of multiple, overlapped circle petals. These blooms were basted only, not yet sewn. Modern ones inspired by that rose have blossomed in several contemporary Albums. Sticky-paper circle templates (1" office dots from an office supply store) simplify the construction,

Left side of center flower for petal placement. ►

PATTERN #11: "Basket of Quarter Roses and Buds"

Second page

and Melody Bollay has given the rose a certain realistic perspective in this graphically easy block. The basket is even easier to make than the rose. The whole block is so appealing that it would enhance any album.

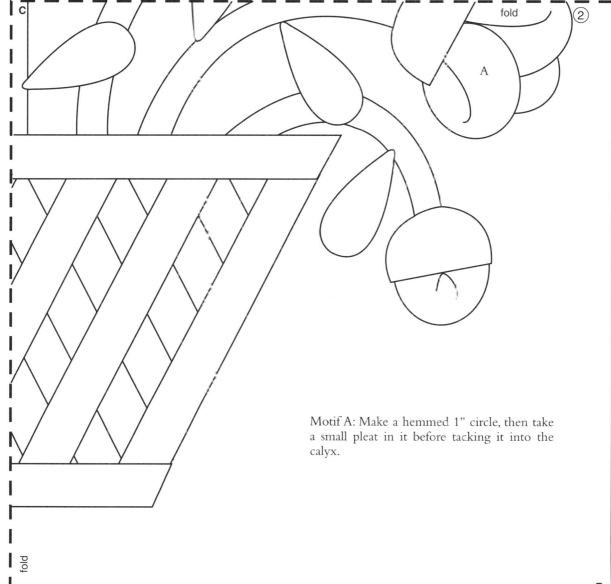

Motif A: Make a hemmed 1" circle, then take a small pleat in it before tacking it into the calyx.

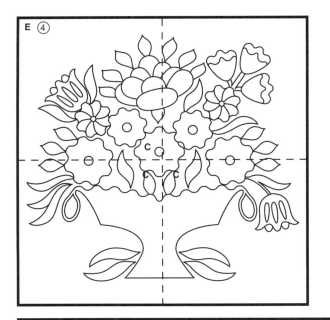

PATTERN #12: "Unadorned Victorian Basket of Flowers"

Type: classic "Baltimore"

To make this block, refer to *Volume I*, Lessons 5 and 10.

This design appears in the classic Album, inscribed "Ladies of Baltimore." It is the simplest of baskets, one of those made from a single piece of cloth. But how cleverly and how clearly Victorian is its style! The flowers are simple. Yet the block itself fits beautifully into any Album, old or new. Learning from old Baltimore, Marsha Carter incorporates tie-dyes (ombre-like) to add a bit of depth to the flat shapes, and fools one's sense of time by adding an antique yellow calico.

Use these blooms in place of 'A' on the right side.

Make flower pattern on fold. ►

fold

A.

fold

C

PATTERN #12: "Unadorned Victorian Basket of Flowers"

Second Page

③ fold

B.

Use this bloom in place of 'B' on right side.

E

C

fold

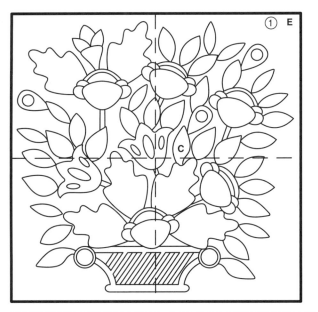

PATTERN #14: "Folk Art Basket of Flowers"

Type: classic "Baltimore"; from Quilt #3 in Baltimore Album Quilts – Historic Notes and Antique Patterns

To make this block, refer to *Volume I*, Lessons 5 and 10.

In this antique quilt, three blocks in a row echo a folk style that we tend to think of as Pennsylvania Dutch or "Deutsch" (which of course means Pennsylvania German). Great numbers of Germans had emigrated to Baltimore by the mid-nineteenth century, and their influence in the Albums was noted by Dr. William Rush Dunton, Jr. The caricatured rose in this bouquet recurs repeatedly in red, yellow, and blue in these classic blocks. Over and over, one sees this color trio on linked cornucopias, baskets, stars, and flowers. Their combination seems significant.

PATTERN #14: "Folk Art Basket of Flowers"

Second page

The Oddfellow and Rebekah's fraternal colors are now red, white, and blue. For the Oddfellows and Rebekahs, the color symbolism of yellow is Friendship, red is Love, and blue is Truth. In this block the buds and blossoms are all red and yellow, the basket a shade of blue. Their specific emblems (the three-linked chain and the five-pointed star-on-point) are always colored red, yellow, and blue in the classic Album Quilts.

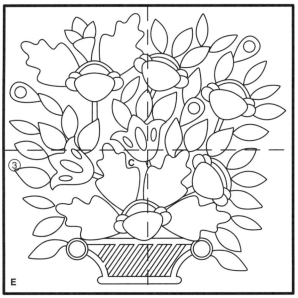

PATTERN #14: "Folk Art Basket of Flowers"

Third Page

In those old quilts, yellow may have been substituted for white to preserve the secrecy so in vogue with those orders. Or perhaps they used yellow consistently to distinguish the symbol from the quilt's white background cloth. This basket's bouquet has a distinctively square profile. In their gravity-defying arrangement, the blooms imitate the stenciled balance of theorem paintings. Traditionally, then as now, we quiltmakers stitch eclectic folk arts of early times into our quilts.

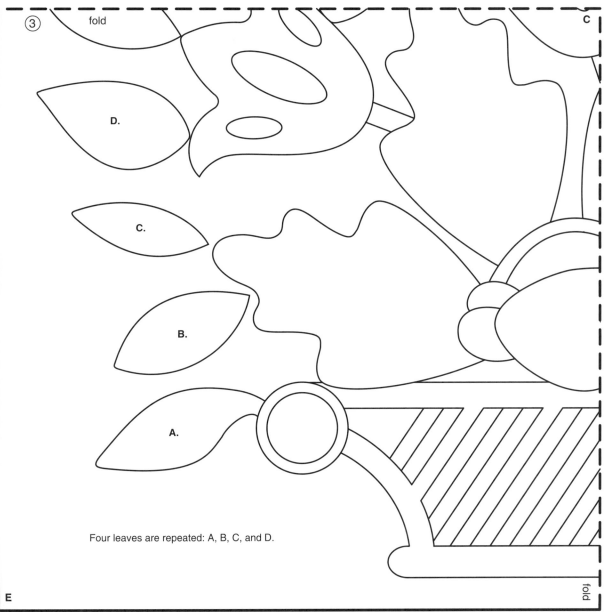

Four leaves are repeated: A, B, C, and D.

PATTERN #14: "Folk Art Basket of Flowers"

Fourth page

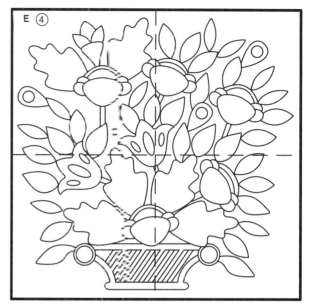

PATTERN #15: "Apples in the Late Afternoon"

Type: "Beyond"; Designed by the author

To make this block, refer to *Volume I*, Lesson 10.

The basket's tie-dyed fabric foundation gives this block the effect of mottled afternoon light. Hence its name. Some blocks sit at the back of your mind for a long time. Then, when you finally get down to making them, both the design and construction come quickly. This is such a block and its making marked a happy memory. The country inn inked in the lower left-hand corner commemorates the anniversary weekend there, when it was finished. Black Pigma .01 permanent pen was used to embellish the block's leaf veins and apple stem-wells. Hand-dyes were used for the appliques.

PATTERN #15: "Apples in the Late Afternoon"

Type: "Beyond"; Designed by the author

The apples that are two-toned have had one side appliquéd out of 1 ½"-wide shaded wire ribbon (with the wire removed). On the apples the shaded ribbon overlay is stuffed. The basket is braided with ⅓"-wide raw-edged bias strips cut from a large print. You could cut these strips with a rotary cutter. For a slightly frayed edge I scissors-cut on either side of ¼" masking tape pressed onto the cloth's true bias. When I peeled the tape off, the cloth edges frayed ever so lightly.

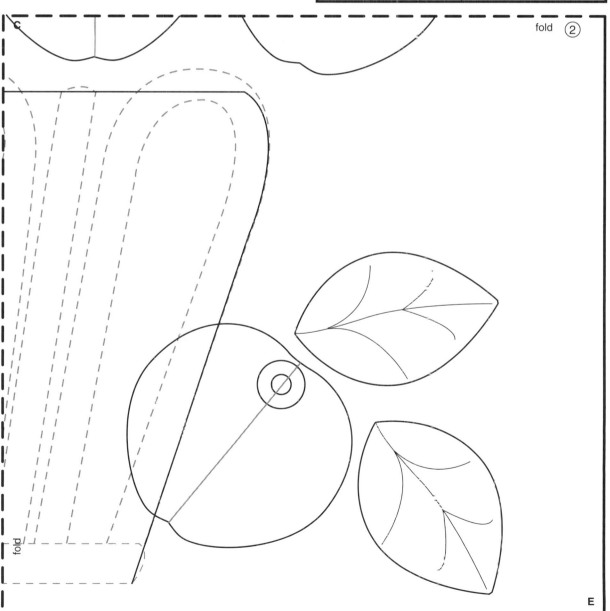

PATTERN #15: "Apples in the Late Afternoon"

Third page

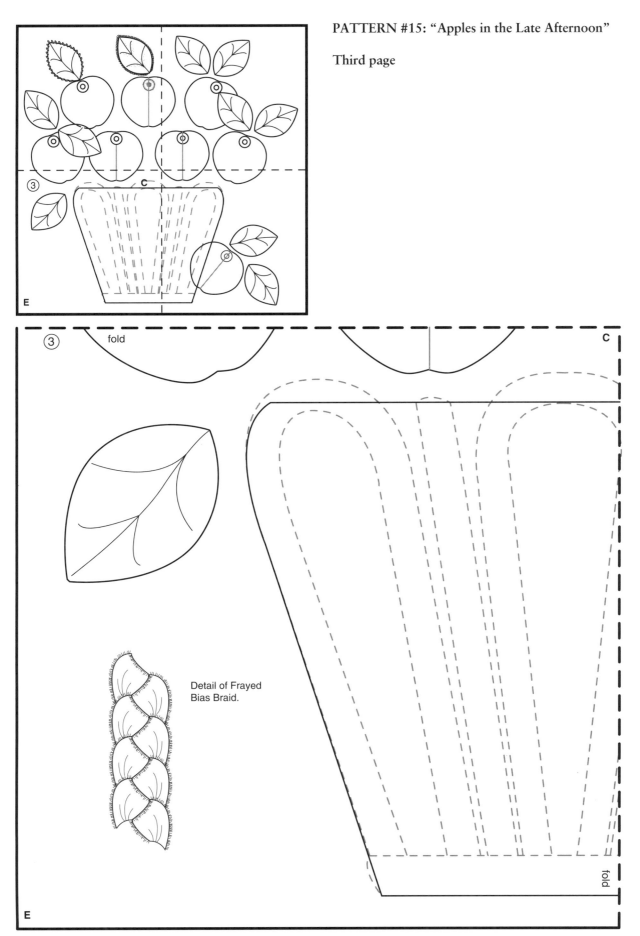

③ fold

C

Detail of Frayed
Bias Braid.

fold

E

PATTERN #15: "Apples in the Late Afternoon"

Fourth page

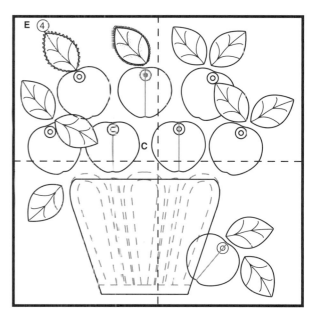

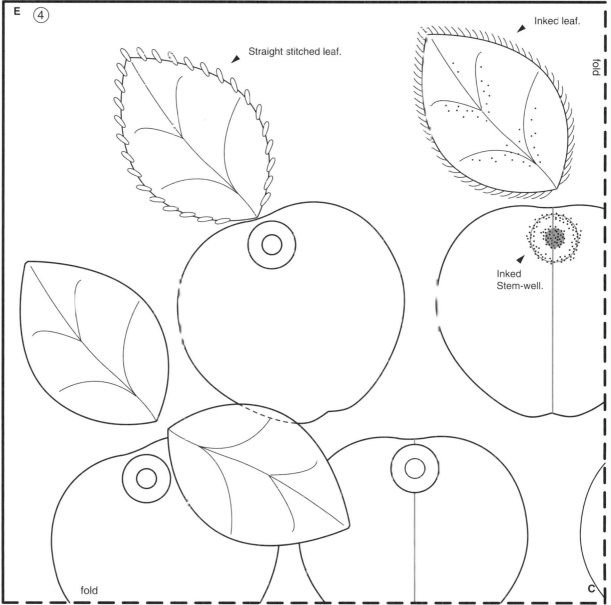

Straight stitched leaf.

Inked leaf.

fold

Inked
Stem-well.

fold

C

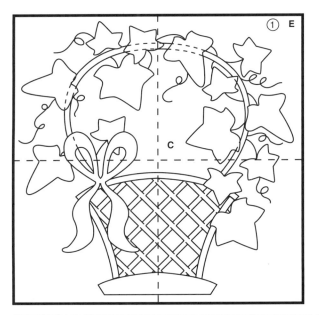

PATTERN #16: "Ivy Basket with Bow"

Type: "Beyond"; Designed by Irene Keating

To make this block, refer to *Volume I*, Lessons 1, 2, and 10.

A simple paper-folded basket shape, a graphic weave, and some pertly tied ivy (wound topiary-like around the handle) make this block both striking and unique. Irene sewed the basket's lattice pattern from one piece of cloth, by cut-away applique. Skill and patience are needed to sew all those sharp inside corners as beautifully as Irene has done. The same basket weave could more easily be done with pre-turned bias stems – layered, edged, and bracketed by base and brim. Irene brought photocopies of ivy leaves from her garden to this block's design session. She shares her charming stylization of those leaves here along with her basket pattern.

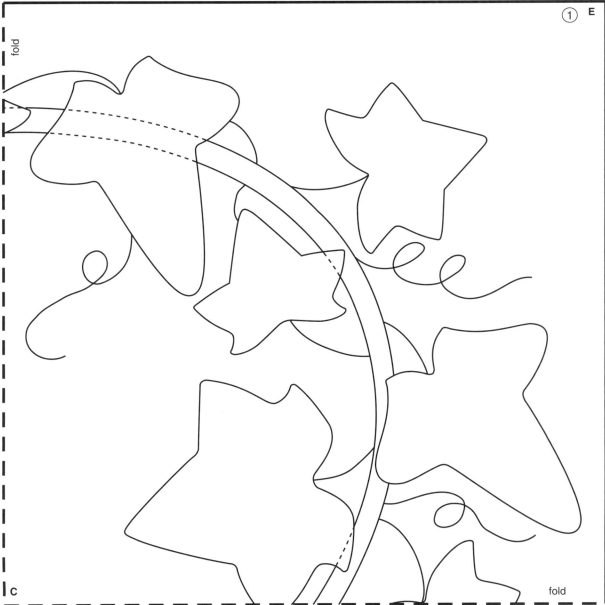

PATTERN #16: "Ivy Basket with Bow"

Second page

Baltimore Beauties Fabric Notes: Two of the monochromatic Vermiculate prints would combine well for this basket. Leaves cut from the "hand-dyed" Baltimore Rose print would make wonderful ivy foliage. This print has the richest, darkest greens, then soft-transitions into sunlit patches where the color lightens dramatically.

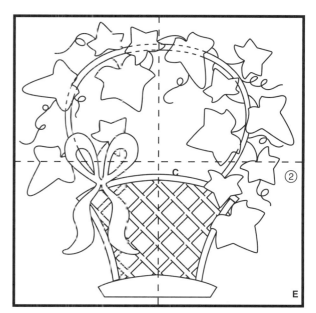

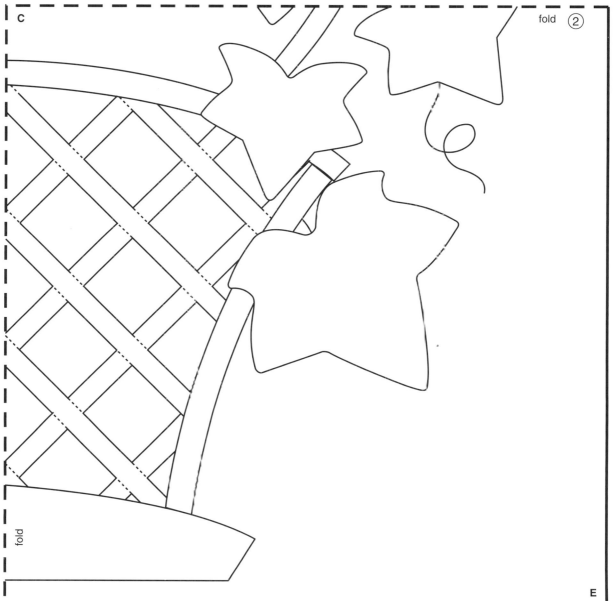

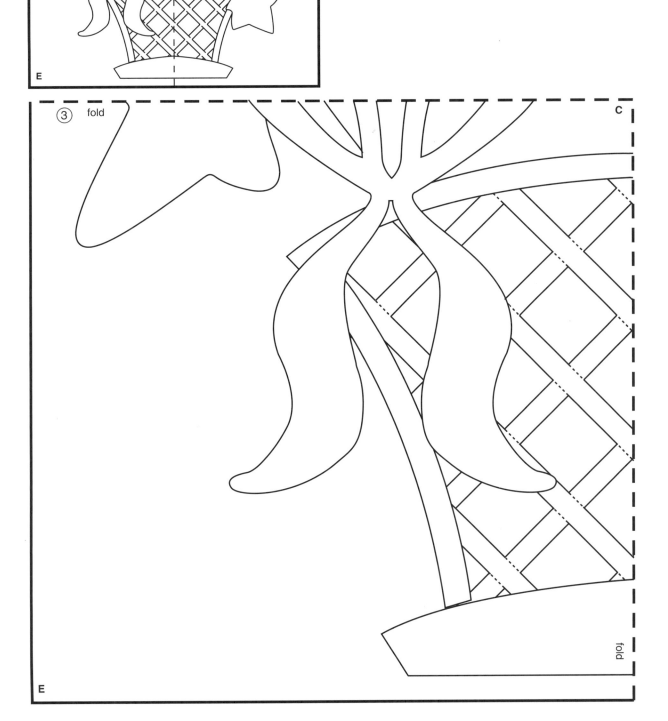

PATTERN #16: "Ivy Basket with Bow"

Third page

PATTERN #16: "Ivy Basket with Bow"

Fourth page

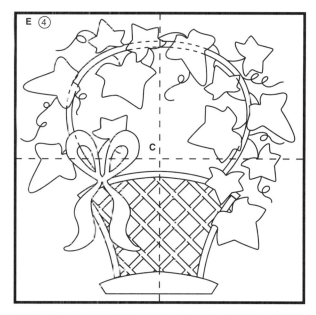

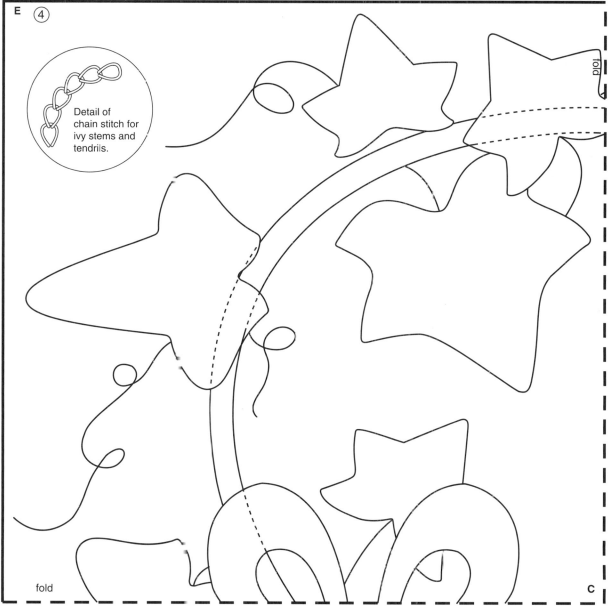

Detail of chain stitch for ivy stems and tendrils.

fold

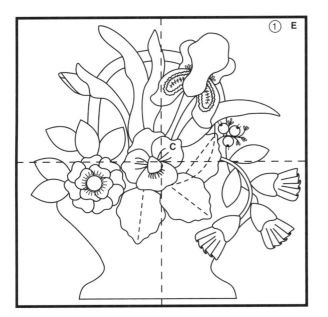

PATTERN #17: "Jeannie's Iris, Pansy, and Pleated Flowers Basket"

Type: "Beyond"; Designed by Jeannie Austin (with Raenell Doyle's basket)

To make this block, refer to *Volume I*, Lessons 9 and 10.

The simplest of baskets—a one-piece shape—and a freshly picked spring bouquet, make this block endearing. Jeannie Austin's strong individual style sings when one is privileged to see numbers of her pieces. Some of that song can be caught here. Jeannie's colors, both delicate and vibrant, also have a special style that draw us to them. And she has characteristic details that, shared here in this pattern, will enter our late-twentieth century Albums. The tiny embroidery accented blueberries recur in her bouquets as do judiciously thread-decorated floral elements.

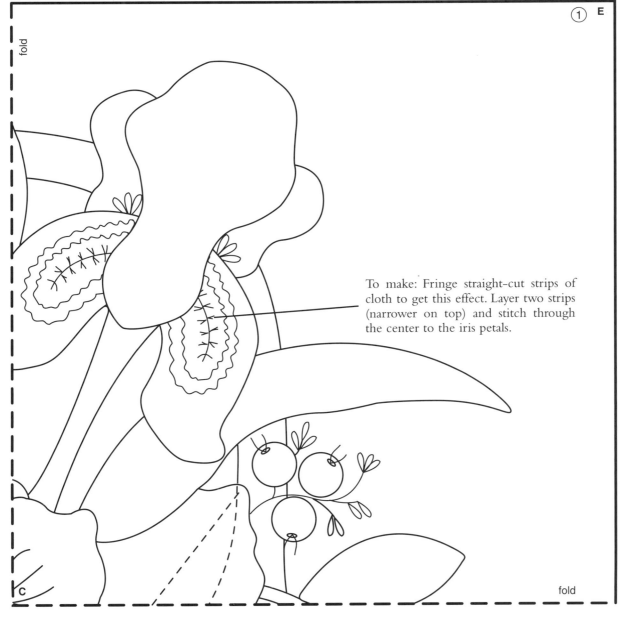

To make: Fringe straight-cut strips of cloth to get this effect. Layer two strips (narrower on top) and stitch through the center to the iris petals.

PATTERN #17: "Jeannie's Iris, Pansy, and Pleated Flowers Basket"

Second page

Jeannie's iris sports a lush beard: double-layered, fringed (raw-edged) bias strips have been gathered down their length and attached to the petal with looped sewing thread. Just by studying the pattern, one can almost picture banks of these sherbet-colored hybrid "flags," which reappear each Spring, full of new life and joyful promise. Jeannie attributes her basket shape to Raenell Doyle, a friend and teacher.

Trace the basket pattern off first, marking half of it on a sheet of paper folded in half lengthwise. Then cut the basket out on the fold. Use a basket print for the applique fabric. Jeannie's pattern shapes and arrangements are simple enough to be machine sewn.

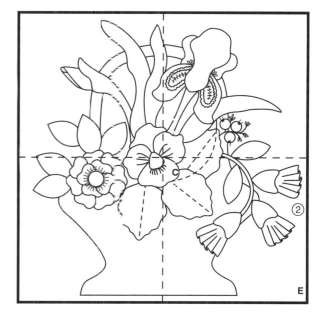

Make pleated blooms.

See instructions for Pleated Flowers on page 77.

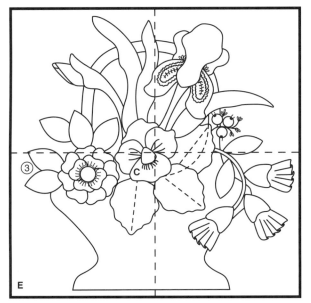

PATTERN #17: "Jeannie's Iris, Pansy, and Pleated Flowers Basket"

Third page

Her basket, leaves, and stems could be mock hand-appliqued (see Harriet Hargrave's *Mastering Machine Applique, 2nd Ed.*). Then one could have the pleasure of doing the flowers and embellishments by hand. Consider this time economizer if you choose to pair this Iris basket pattern with Jeannie's "Regal Bird" basket as an elegant set of boudoir or parlor pictures or pillows.

PATTERN #17: "Jeannie's Iris, Pansy, and Pleated Flowers Basket"

Fourth page

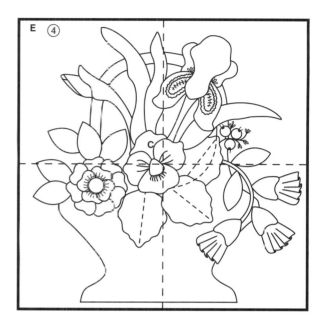

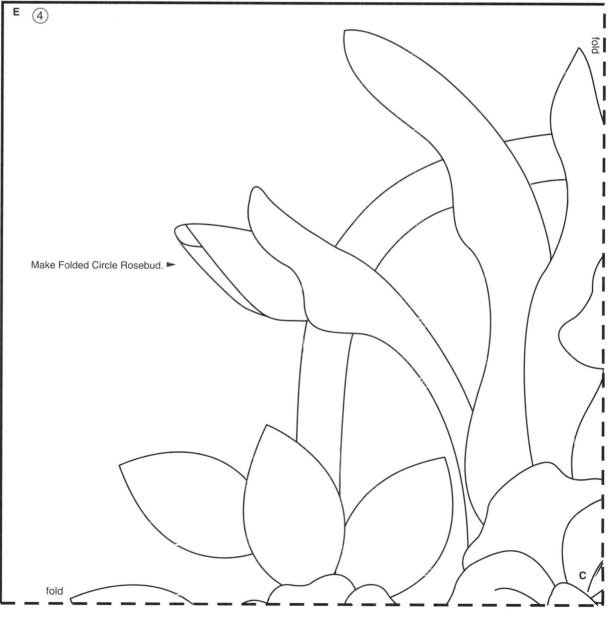

Make Folded Circle Rosebud. ►

fold

fold

E ④

C

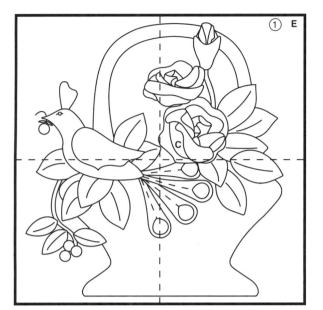

PATTERN #18: "Regal Bird Amidst the Roses"

Type: "Beyond"; Designed by Jeanie Austin (with Raenell Doyle's basket)

To make this block, refer to *Volume I*, Lessons 5, 9, and 10.

Using the same Raenell Doyle–inspired basket shape, Jeannie has designed a block that is slightly more formal than the preceding "Iris, Pansy, and Pleated Flowers." While the basket shape and construction remain utterly simple, the arrangement in the basket has a more formal elegance to it. The fulsome dimensional roses, the regally exotic peacock, and the studied, artful placement of bird and blooms within the basket

fold

Centers of Roses are Folded Circle Rosebuds.

C

fold

① E

PATTERN #18: "Regal Bird Amidst the Roses"

Second Page

all conspire to make a most appealing nouvelle Victorian pattern. And it is a relatively easy one at that! For those of us who enjoy original design, this concept of repeating the basic graphic basket shape, but changing the arrangement in each, might lead to a basket Album based on a similarly consistent theme.

Background fabrics sometimes change in the antique Albums. (One memorable antebellum block has a square of wee rosebuds behind the appliquéd image, then a narrow border of plain off-white fabric frames it.) This variety adds interest to an Album. Why not use a painterly selection of background fabrics? Emphatic, simpler appliqué shapes like this block's motifs show

fold ②

C

fold

E

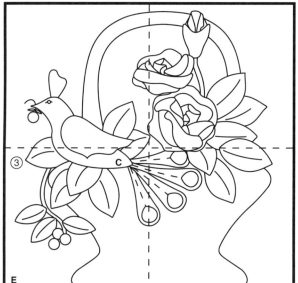

PATTERN #18: "Regal Bird Amidst the Roses"

Third Page

dramatically against a print-enriched background—inside your Album, beside it in a frilled or prairie-point edged pillow, or framed, Victoriana-like, on the wall above.

PATTERN #18: "Regal Bird Amidst the Roses"

Fourth Page

PATTERN #21: "Baltimore Bouquet"

Type: "Beyond"; Designed by Gwendolyn LaLecheur

To make this block, refer to *Volume I*, Lessons 5, 8, and 10.

Gwen suggests this approach to her block:

1. Applique the bow and all the leaves except the gathered leaves, which lie under the ruched roses.
2. Ruched roses.
3. Yo-Yos: Trace around a large spool of thread onto fabric. Cut out with a ¼" seam allowance. Turn the raw edge to the wrong side on the drawn line. Stitch this hem with small running stitches. Pull thread to gather and backstitch to hold the gathers.

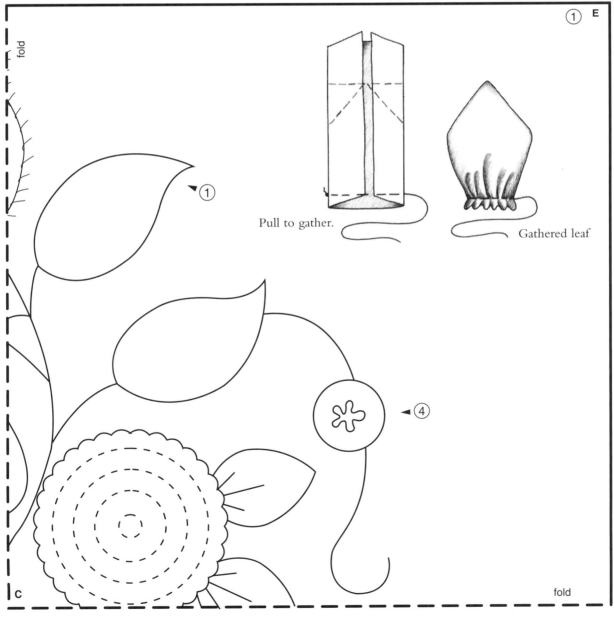

Pull to gather.

Gathered leaf

PATTERN #21: "Baltimore Bouquet"

Second Page

Stitch through the yo-yo's center with matching thread to sew it to the background. Tuck in a fringed center.
4. Petals-on-a-String, instructions follow on third and fourth pages of pattern.

1. Stem Stitch 2. Petals-on-a-String
3. Gathered Leaves 4. Yo-Yo Posey
5. Ruched Rose 6. Blanket-Stitched Leaves
7. French Knots 8. Triple Bowknot Ribbon

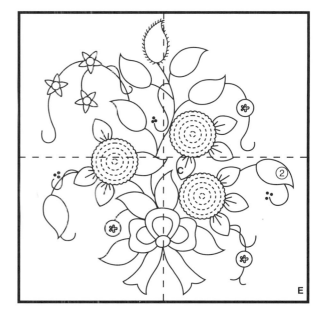

PATTERN #21: "Baltimore Bouquet"

Third Page

Gwen's Gathered Leaves:
1. Cut a bias strip 2" wide and 9" long. Run the strip through a 1" bias-tape maker to fold the raw edges under.
2. Cut the bias strip into three 3" lengths. To make a leaf, finger-press a 1" hem at the top end of the leaf. Fold the left and right edges into the center as if making a prairie point.
3. Gather along the bottom edge. Secure the stitches. Trim off the excess fabric at bottom. Appliqué with seam-side down.

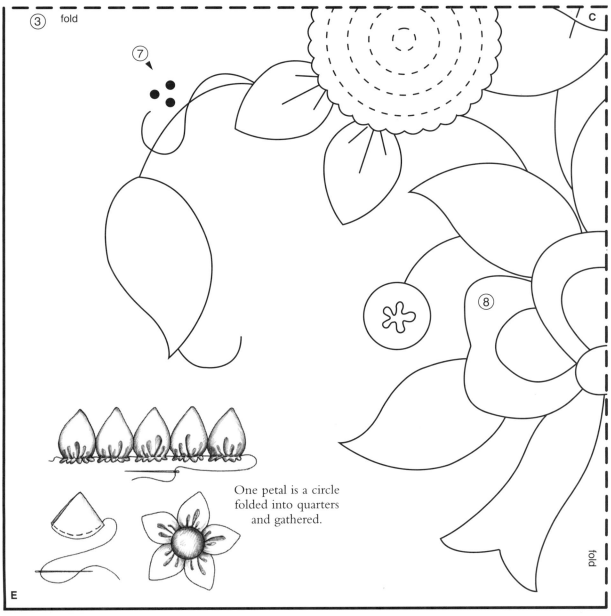

One petal is a circle folded into quarters and gathered.

PATTERN #21: "Baltimore Bouquet"

Fourth Page

Petals-on-a-String:
1. Trace around a quarter or other round object. Cut out a circle on this drawn line.
2. Fold the circle (right sides out) into quarters.
3. Sew close to the raw edges through all the layers. Do not cut the thread. Make another circle. Repeat steps 1 and 2, then add this petal onto the string (Figure 8.5).
4. Make a total of five circles. Draw them into a circle, connecting the first and the last petal. Secure the thread. The fold of each petal should be on the same side. Sew in place along the inside leaving the petals free. Fill the centers with an appliquéd circle.

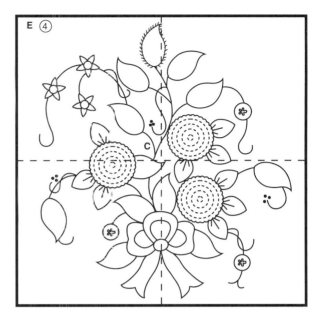

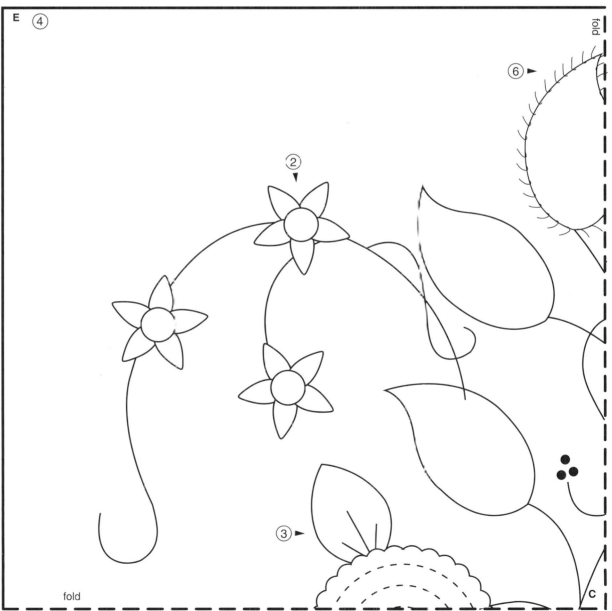

PATTERN #27: "Pedestal Basket with Handle"

Type: "Beyond"; Designed by the author

Three stems twist to form the brim's valley, then extend to braided handles on this basket. The braided vertical handle is optional and would best be sewn down after the basket is filled so that it passes over, then appears to go behind, the contents.

Continue the braid in an arc to form the handle.

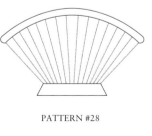

PATTERN #27

PATTERN #28: "Annie Tuley's Pleated Basket"

Type: "Beyond"; Designed by Annie Tuley

This effective basket was made with Clotilde's Perfect Pleater®.

PATTERN #28

PATTERN #33

PATTERN #33: "Kaye's Ribbon Basket*"

Type: "Beyond"; Designed by Kaye Stafford

Pattern #32: "Ribbonwork Basket for *Broiderie Perse* Blooms"

Type: "Beyond"; Designed by the author

For A, twist two different shades of ⅝"-wide satin ribbon together.
For B, braid three shades of ¼"-wide satin ribbon together.

PATTERN #32

LEAFY BORDER.

Enlarge 135% for original
size for a 6" border.

Two Borders

These borders are called center-running borders because a motif is continuously repeated along the border's center length. Edging patterns are presented on pages 133-136 in *The Best of Baltimore Beauties*. These motifs can be reduced or enlarged on a copying machine to fit any border size.

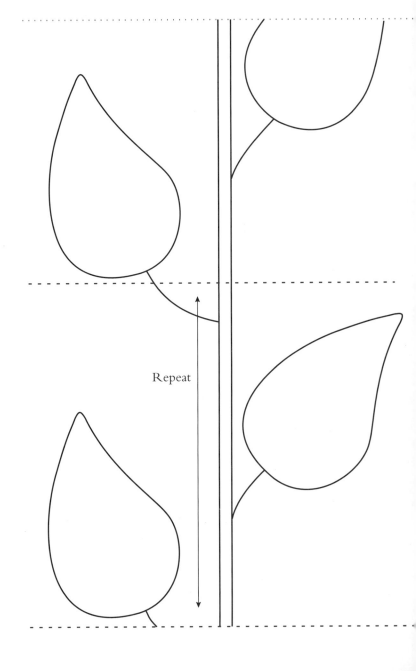

Repeat

South of Baltimore
by Patricia Jane West, 2001.

The gardens and writings of Thomas Jefferson inspired this quilt. "I spent my early quilting years in Virginia and visited Monticello many times. The original border design was based on bracelets that have been in the family since 1850—coincidentally, the beginning of the Baltimore Album Quilt era."

PATTERN 1:
Heart Wreath of Roses
by Mary K. Tozer, 2001.

PATTERN 2:
Heart Wreath of Acorns
by Mary K. Tozer, 2001.

PATTERN 3:
Heart Wreath of Cherries
by Melinda K. Hiles, 2001.

PATTERN 4:
Heart Wreath of Tulips
by Arden Macy, 2001

Precious Memories
A Baltimore Album Quilt by Anne Connery, 88" x 98", 1990-1998.

My Baltimore Album quilt was begun in a year-long Block-a-Month Class at Seminole Sampler in Catonsville, Maryland, in 1990. This class, taught by Mimi Dietrich, covered the lessons in *Baltimore Beauties and Beyond, Vol. I*, by Elly Sienkiewicz. I created Precious Memories to honor and celebrate the women in my life, especially my mother and grandmother. Nancy Ogletree hand quilted my album.

PATTERN 5:
Baltimore Rose Bouquet
by Cynthia Williford, 2002.

PATTERN 5:
Baltimore Rose Bouquet
by Patty Henry, 2001.

PATTERN 6:
Baltimore Basket of Roses
by Jayne Slovick, 2002.

PATTERN 7:
Baltimore Urn of Roses
by Cynthia Williford, 2001.

PATTERN 8:
Squared Wreath of
Embroidered Flowers
by Marjorie Mahoney, 2001.

PATTERN 9:
Intertwined Crown of Flowers
by Nancy Kerns, 2002.

Odense Album
A group quilt designed by and made under the direction of Elly Sienkiewicz in honor of
Hans Christian Anderson. Border appliqué by Albertine Veenstra, quilting by Mona
Cumberledge, 70" x 70", 1989–1990.

Album in Honor of Mother, group quilt designed by and made under the direction of Elly Sienkiewicz, 81" x 81", appliquéd and set 1990–92, quilted by Mona Cumberledge 1996-97. Center medallion by Barbara Hahl and Yolanda Tovar, borders by Sylvia Pickell and Ruth Meyers (who also set and edged the quilt.)

Heart-Garlanded Album, group quilt made under the direction of Elly Sienkiewicz, quilted by Genevieve A. Greco, 87" x 87",1992–93. Photo by J. Mathieson

The Baltimore Beauties Album, group quilt designed by and made under the direction of Elly Sienkiewicz, 95" x 95", 1988–1993.

Ruth Meyers appliquéd and embroidered the border, the center block, and set the quilt together. She worked the border while living in Saudi Arabia during Desert Storm. The sashing is by Audrey Waite, quilted by Mona Cumberledge and Joyce Hill.

PATTERN 12:
Theorem-Style Urn of Flowers
by Bette Florette Augustine, 2002.

PATTERN 11:
Grape-Flanked Urn of Fruit
by Lynn A. Thurston, 2002.

Repeat

Repeat

Leaf #2

Leaf #1

GRAPEVINE BORDER.

Enlarge 150% for original
size for a 10" border.

Flop the repeat as needed
to make your border the
desired length.

PATTERN #1: Kangaroos

Type: Beyond Baltimore. Designed by the author.

To make this block, refer to *Volume I*, Lesson 1 or 2.

PATTERN #2: Varietal Fleur-de-Lis I

Type: Beyond Baltimore

To make this block, refer to *Volume I*, Lesson 1 or 2.

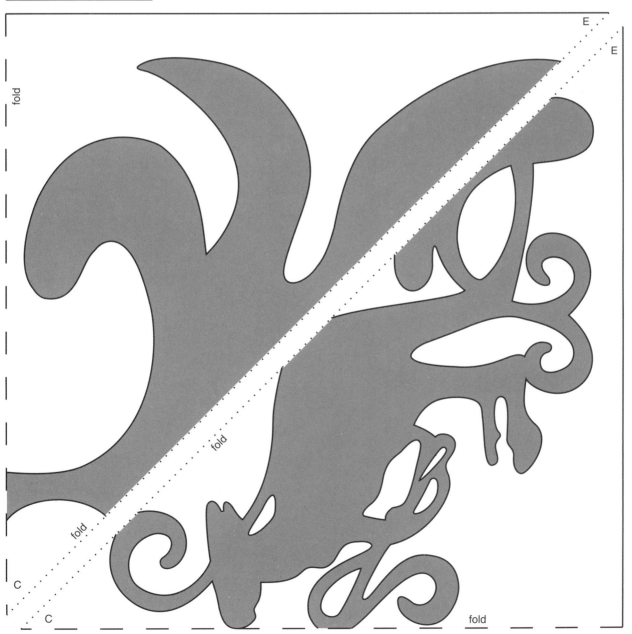

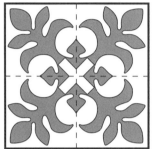

PATTERN #5: Varietal Botanical I

Type: Beyond Baltimore

To make this block, refer to *Volume I*, Lesson 1 or 2.

PATTERN #6: Varietal Fleur-de-Lis II

Type: Beyond Baltimore

To make this block, refer to *Volume I*, Lesson 1 or 2.

PATTERN #7: Varietal Fleur–de–Lis III

Type: Beyond Baltimore

To make this block, refer to *Volume I*, Lesson 1 or 2.

PATTERN #8: Varietal Botanical III

Type: Beyond Baltimore

To make this block, refer to *Volume I*, Lesson 1 or 2.

PATTERN #9: Varietal Botanical III

Type: Beyond Baltimore

To make this block, refer to *Volume I*, Lesson 1 or 2.

PATTERN #10: Varietal Botanical IV

Type: Beyond Baltimore

To make this block, refer to *Volume I*, Lesson 1 or 2.

PATTERN #15: Varietal Fleur-de-Lis IV

Type: Beyond Baltimore

To make this block, refer to *Volume I*, Lesson 1 or 2.

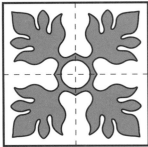

PATTERN #16: Varietal Botanical V

Type: Beyond Baltimore

To make this block, refer to *Volume I*, Lesson 1 or 2.

PATTERN #17: Varietal Botanical VI

Type: Beyond Baltimore

To make this block, refer to *Volume I*, Lesson 1 or 2.

PATTERN #18: Varietal Botanical VII

Type: Beyond Baltimore

To make this block, refer to *Volume I*, Lesson 1 or 2.

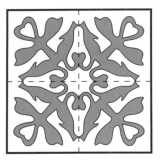

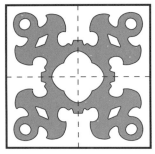

PATTERN #19: Hearts and Swans

Type: Beyond Baltimore. Contemporary design by Pat Gallagher.

To make this block, refer to *Volume I*, Lesson 1 or 2.

PATTERN #20: Abstract Design I

Type: Beyond Baltimore

To make this block, refer to *Volume I*, Lesson 1 or 2.

PATTERN #23: Varietal Botanical VIII

Type: Beyond Baltimore

To make this block, refer to *Volume I*, Lesson 1 or 2.

PATTERN #24: Varietal Botanical IX

Type: Beyond Baltimore

To make this block, refer to *Volume I*, Lesson 1 or 2.

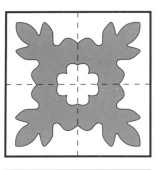

PATTERN #27: Varietal Botanical X

Type: Beyond Baltimore. This is the logo of the Continental Quilting Congress, a contemporary design by Hazel Carter.

To make this block, refer to *Volume I*, Lesson 1 or 2.

PATTERN #28: Abstract Design II

Type: Beyond Baltimore

To make this block, refer to *Volume I*, Lesson 1 or 2.

PATTERN #29: Varietal Fleur-de-Lis V

Type: Beyond Baltimore

To make this block, refer to *Volume I*, Lesson 1 or 2.

PATTERN #30: Varietal Botanical XI

Type: Beyond Baltimore

To make this block, refer to *Volume I*, Lesson 1 cr 2.

PATTERN #31: Varietal Fleur-de-Lis VI

Type: Beyond Baltimore

To make this block, refer to *Volume I*, Lesson 1 or 2.

PATTERN #32: Varietal Botanical XII

Type: Beyond Baltimore

To make this block, refer to *Volume I*, Lesson 1 or 2.

PATTERN #35: Pineapple

Type: Baltimore-style

To make this block, refer to *Volume I*, Lesson 1 or 2.

PATTERN #36: Alex's Cats

Type: Beyond Baltimore. Designed by the author for Classic Revival: Alex's Album. ("A" for Alex Sits between these cats.)

To make this block, refer to *Volume I*, Lesson 1 or 2.

PATTERN #39: Varietal Fleur-de-Lis VII

Type: Classic Baltimore, from the Album inscribed "Seidenstricker," "Baltimore," and "1845."

To make this block, refer to *Volume I*, Lesson 1 or 2.

PATTERN #40: Varietal Botanical XIII

Type: Classic Baltimore, from the Album inscribed "Seidenstricker," "Baltimore," and "1845."

To make this block, refer to *Volume I*, Lesson 1 or 2.

PATTERN #45: Turtle Hill

Type: Beyond Baltimore. Designed by the author for Classic Revival: Alex's Album.

To make this block, refer to *Volume I*, Lesson 1 or 2. Cut the paper template for this block as a four-repeat pattern.

PATTERN #47: Carnations

Type: Beyond Baltimore. Designed by the author for Classic Revival: Alex's Album.

To make this block, refer to *Volume I*, Lesson 1 or 2.

PATTERN #48: Double Hearts

Type: Classic Baltimore. Occurs in the Baltimore Museum of Art's Mary Everist Album among others.

To make this block, refer to *Volume I*, Lesson 1 or 2.

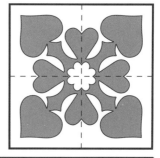

PATTERN #49: Rose Medallion

Type: Beyond Baltimore

To make this block, refer to *Volume I*, Lesson 1 or 2.

PATTERN #50: Great Grandma May Ross Hamilton's Scottish Thistle

Type: Beyond Baltimore. Designed by the author for Classic Revival: Alex's Album.

To make this block, refer to *Volume I*, Lesson 1 or 2.

PATTERN #53: Hearts and Tulips

Type: Classic Baltimore. From a quilt inscribed with Numsen Family names.

To make this block, refer to *Volume I*, Lesson 1 or 2.

PATTERN #54: Landon Bears Football Team

Type: Beyond Baltimore. Designed by the author for Classic Revival: Alex's Album.

To make this block, refer to *Volume I*, Lesson 1 or 2. Cut this block from a paper folded in eighths. Open to fourths to cut the "L" or other letter on the bears' uniform.

PATTERN #57: Pinecones for Maine

Type: Beyond Baltimore. Designed by the author for Classic Revival: Alex's Album.

To make this block, refer to *Volume I*, Lesson 1 or 2.

PATTERN #58: Varietal Botanical XIV

Type: Baltimore-style

To make this block, refer to *Volume I*, Lesson 1 or 2.

PATTERN #59: Christmas Cactus Variation

Type: Baltimore-style

To make this block, refer to *Volume I*, Lesson 1 or 2.

PATTERN #60: Varietal Botanical XV

Type: Baltimore-style

To make this block, refer to *Volume I*, Lesson 1 or 2.

PATTERN #61: Varietal Fleur-de-Lis VIII

Type: Baltimore-style

To make this block, refer to *Volume I*, Lesson 1 or 2.

PATTERN #62: Varietal Fleur-de-Lis IX

Type: Classic Baltimore. From a quilt inscribed "1850."

To make this block, refer to *Volume I*, Lesson 1 or 2.

PATTERN #63: Sometimes Take Tea

Type: Beyond Baltimore. Designed by Kathryn Blomgren Campbell for Bonnie's Album.

To make this block, refer to *Volume I*, Lesson 1 or 2. On the pattern, remove the spout from the left side of each teapot at the dashed lines.

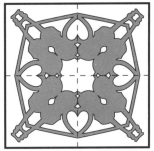

PATTERN #64: Violins and Bows

Type: Beyond Baltimore. Designed by Kathryn Blomgren Campbell for Bonnie's Album.

To make this block, refer to *Volume I*, Lesson 1 or 2.

PATTERN #65: Flamingos

Type: Beyond Baltimore. Designed by Kathryn Blomgren Campbell for Lindsay's Album.

To make this block, refer to *Volume I*, Lesson 1 or 2.

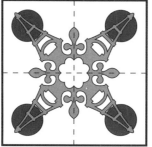

PATTERN #66: Eiffel Tower

Type: Beyond Baltimore. Designed by Kathryn Blomgren Campbell for Lindsay's Album.

To make this block, refer to *Volume I*, Lesson 1 or 2.

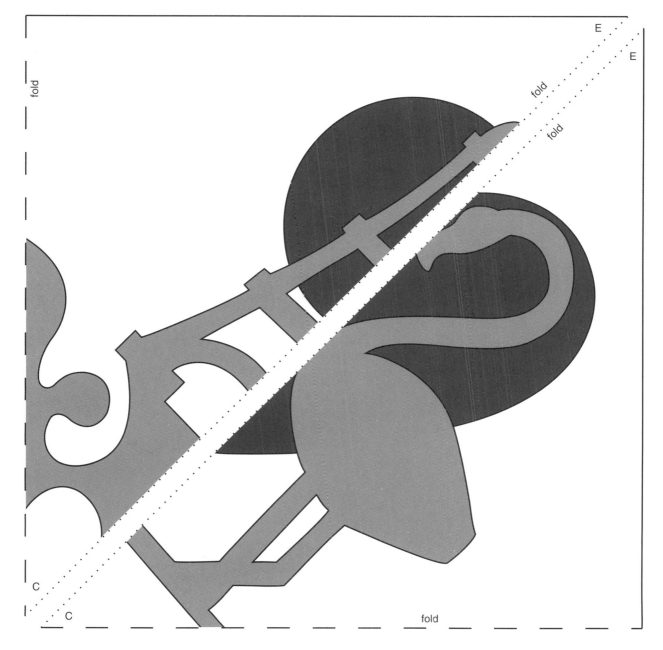

PATTERN #67: Lindsay as a Young Gymnast

Type: Beyond Baltimore. Designed by Kathryn Blomgren Campbell for Lindsay's Album.

To make this block, refer to *Volume I*, Lesson 1 or 2.

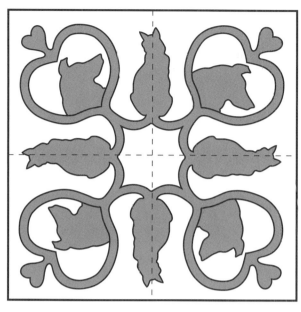

PATTERN #68: Family Pets

Type: Beyond Baltimore. Designed by Jan Sheridan for Remembrance II.

To make this block, refer to *Volume I*, Lesson 1 or 2. Cut four cat and dog templates to tape to the full-size freezer pattern. Place these so that all the dogs face clockwise and all the cats face counter-clockwise.

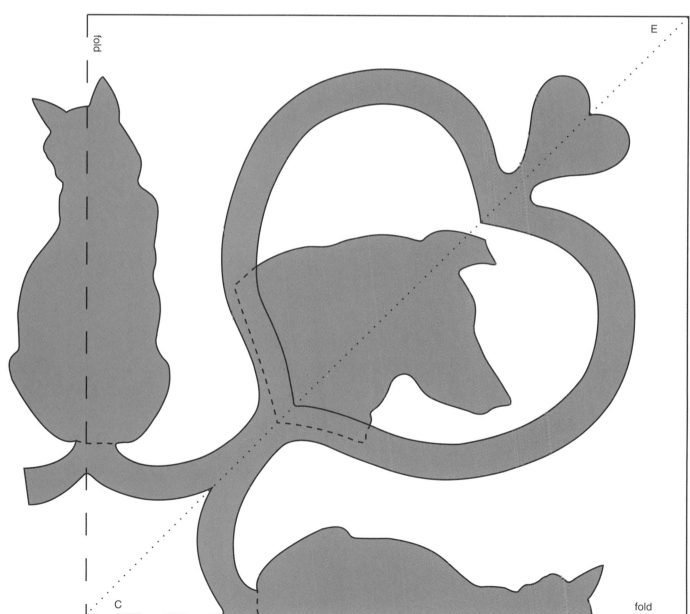

PATTERN #69: Tiptoe Through My Tulips

Type: Beyond Baltimore. Designed by Gwendolyn LeLacheur.

To make this block, refer to *Volume I*, Lessons 5 and 10.

Reminiscent of classic Baltimore, this is a simpler block, which would liven any Album. Gwen used the superfine stem method for the tulip stems, chain-stitch (with two strands of embroidery floss) for the berry stems, and needleturn with freezer paper on the top for both the center frame and the floral appliques. The center space is just waiting for a benevolent inscription!

Detail of Chain Stitch

E

fold

fold

C

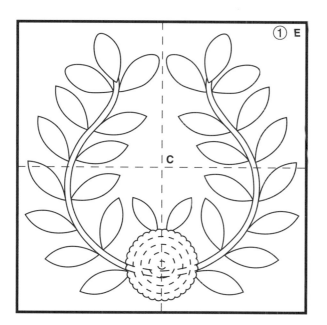

PATTERN #70: Ruched Ribbon Rose Lyre II

Type: Beyond Baltimore

To make this block, refer to *Volume I*, Lessons 2, 5, 8, 9, and 10.

Pattern from a mid-nineteenth century Pennsylvania Album. The pattern Ruched Rose Lyre is included in Volume I. There, it bears a note saying that I had seen a similar block pictured in a quilt, but having been unable to relocate the photo, I'd recreated that Volume I pattern from memory. This second version is a faithful pattern of the antique original pictured in Jane Kolter's *Forget Me Not*. Judy DeCosmo has interpreted the ruching in picot-edged satin ribbon on a spray of country-fresh green geometric cottons. Many such antique Album lyre wreaths are tipped by three red leaves on either side. Were they meant to be rosebuds?

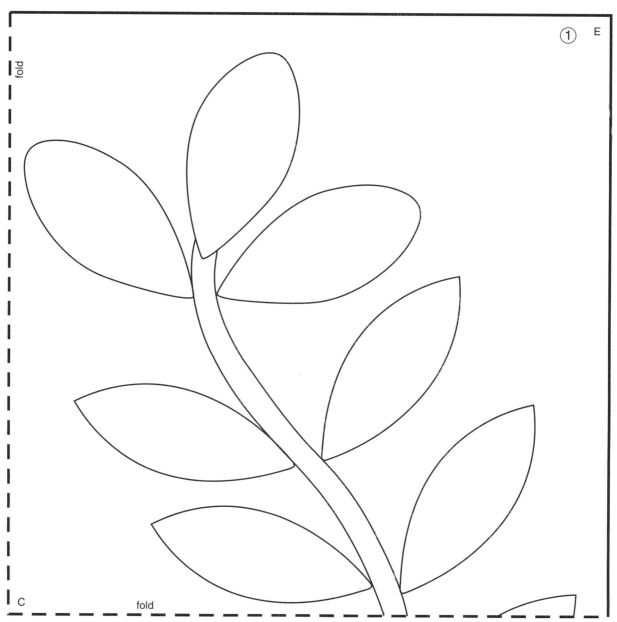

PATTERN #70: Ruched Ribbon Rose Lyre II

Second Page

Or if the wreath is of laurel, could the laurel be wound with roses and buds? The Victorians made an art of mourning the dead. Their culture of piety included repeatedly stitching, carving, and painting eulogies. One can read signs of memento mori in the Album wreaths—whether these be floral wreaths, or heart wreaths and lyre wreaths twined with buds, fruits, and blossoms. Contemporary attitudes toward the dead have differed dramatically from those of Victorian times, but one senses a swing back to those Victorian sensibilities. Then, too, these laudatory wreath symbols can also be sewn for the living who will surely appreciate the approbation!

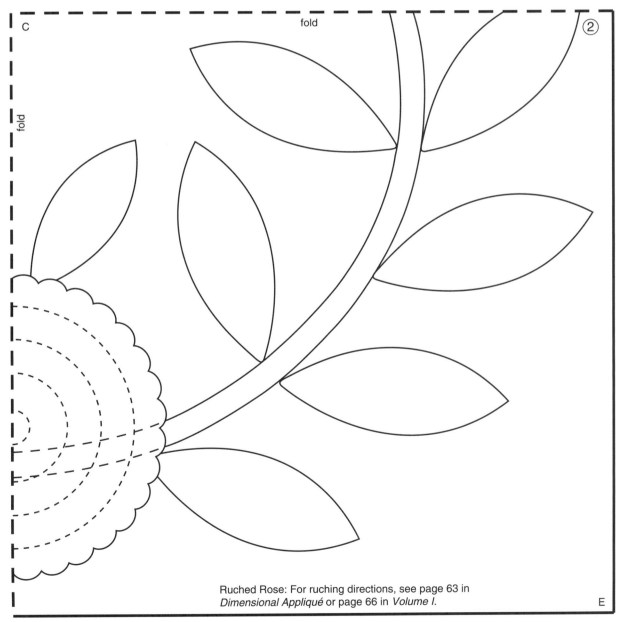

Ruched Rose: For ruching directions, see page 63 in *Dimensional Appliqué* or page 66 in *Volume I.*

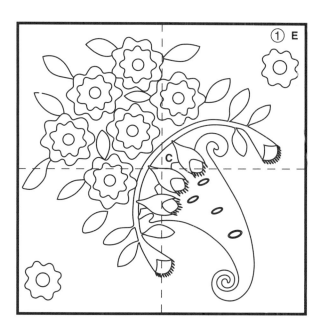

PATTERN # 71: Cornucopia III.

Type: Classic Baltimore

In *Design a Baltimore Album Quilt!* we studied how the appliqué design's shape on a given block can actually help organize the allover interior pattern of an Album Quilt. Blocks set on the diagonal are very useful in this regard, but patterns for them are hard to find. This diagonally placed cornucopia is based on block E-4 in Ladies of Baltimore, Quilt #4 in Baltimore Album Quilt, The Pattern Companion to Volume I. An exceptional

PATTERN #71: Cornucopia III.

Second page

quiltmaker, personalized the pattern a bit by reversing a "W" for her surname into her contemporary reproduction of this block. See color plate 18. Note that this pattern can be oriented on the block to suit your quilt's needs.

PATTERN #71: Cornucopia III.

Third page

PATTERN #71: Cornucopia III.

Fourth page

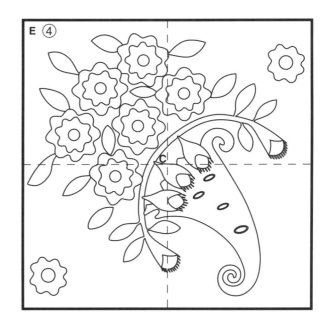

PATTERN #73: Strawberry Wreath III.

Type: Classic Baltimore

To make this block, refer to *Volume 1*, Lessons 5, 7, 9, or 10.

Strawberries, meaning "esteem and love," are twined in a circular wreath, framing, in the prototype block, an ardent dedication. Mary Ann Andrews stitched these fruit into fresh abundance with DMC Medici® wool. This block's original is E-2 in Quilt #3 in *Baltimore Album Quilts, A Pattern Companion to Volume I*. Penned carefully in its center is:

PATTERN #73: Strawberry Wreath III.

Second Page

To the Gray Boys,
Guardians of Freedom, Justice and Virtue
    Citizens, soldiers of Liberty's soil,
This token of Friendship I gladly present you,
    Then guard it from insult and shield it from spoil
Strong be the links in the chain of your union,
    And never the soldier's proud precept forsake;
Long may you live in a martial communion;
    And scorned be the coward who the conflict sent back.
—M.A.B.
(Transcription from Dunton's *Old Quilts*, page 23. Dena Katzenberg's Baltimore Album quilts, page 84, transcribes the last line as "And scorn'd be the slavery who the compact would break.")

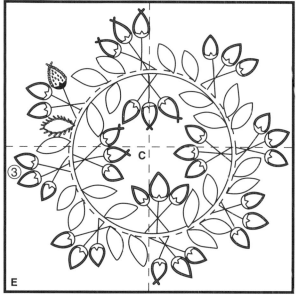

PATTERN #73: Strawberry Wreath III.

Third Page

PATTERN #73: Strawberry Wreath III.

Fourth Page

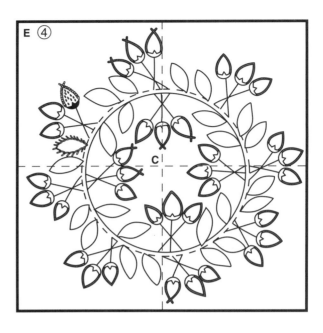

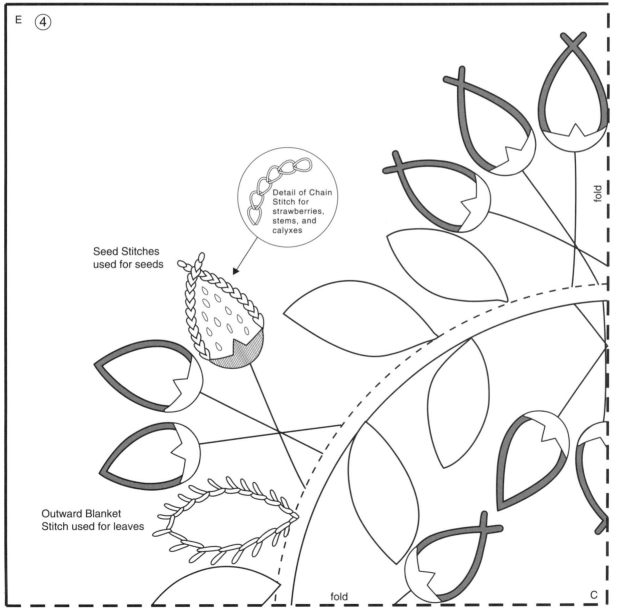

PATTERN #74: Dove and Lyre.

Type: Baltimore-style. (From Quilt #2 in *Volume I*)

To make this block, refer to *Volume I*, Lessons 5 and 10.

This classic block rings the themes we've come to love: doves, lyres, flowers, and wreaths. It has been included to give you yet one more of the ornate Victorian Album Blocks to stitch into rebirth in your Album.

PATTERN #74: Dove and Lyre.

Second page

PATTERN #74: Dove and Lyre.

Third page

PATTERN #74: Dove and Lyre.

Fourth page

PATTERN #75: Album in a Rose Lyre Wreath.

Type: Classic Baltimore. (From Quilt #11 in *Volume II*)

To make this block, refer to Lessons 2 and 10 in *Volume I*.

Books recur repeatedly in Album blocks. "The book," the Bible, was used emblematically by the Odd Fellows to represent "Truth" in their motto "Friendship, Love, and Truth." (Friendship was symbolized by a shepherd's staff and tent, Love by the dove with olive branch.) Books in the old Album Quilts are diversely labeled: Bible, Hymns, Sacred Hymns, Al-

PATTERN #75: Album in a Rose Lyre Wreath.

Second page

bum, and Lady's Album. Entwined in roses, endearing, enduring friendship seems this block's theme. Yvonne Suutari has embroidered this reproduction exquisitely, using white machine-embroidery thread, single strand, to hand-embellish the roses in fine buttonhole stitch. You could ink the decoration and title on the Album, or you could simplify it and embroider it in chain stitch as Yvonne has done. She reverse appliquéd the book's binding.

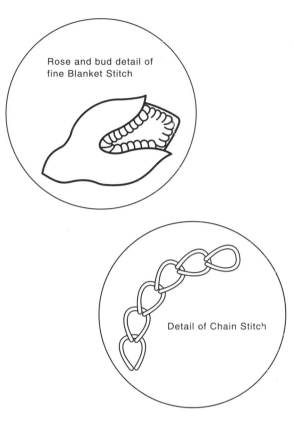

Rose and bud detail of fine Blanket Stitch

Detail of Chain Stitch

DETAILS FROM PATTERN #75: Album in a Rose Lyre Wreath.

Third page

Often in Album Quilts, the books look upside down. For an example, see The Album (Color Plate #24), reproduced by Letty Martin. In such renditions, the writing is right-side up, but the binding and the ribbon bookmarks (often red, yellow, and blue) look appropriate to a book reversed. While we can never be precisely certain what this iconography intends, it occurs with such frequency that I think it may depict the book (the Bible, the friendship Album, the sacred hymnal, the memory Album) opening heavenward for the sweetness of the good spirit to rise therefrom. Frequently, the book is not labeled, leaving us to wonder if the good spirit comes from friendship or from sacred script. But this imagery (like the flowers representing the sweet soul rising from an urn or vase) is one that the ladies of Baltimore were clearly fond of!

PATTERN #77: Victorian Basket of Flowers III.

Type: Baltimore-Style

To make this block, refer to *Volume I*, Lessons 5, 9, and 10. Also see Appendix I in *Baltimore Album Quilts, Pattern Companion to Volume I*.

Yet another extravagant, exquisite classic basket! The pattern has been faithfully drawn from Block B-3 in Quilt #2 in *Volume I*. See that photograph for a full-color model.

PATTERN #77: Victorian Basket of Flowers III.

Second page

PATTERN #77: Victorian Basket of Flowers III.

Third page

PATTERN #77: Victorian Basket of Flowers III.

Fourth page

PATTERN #78: Basket of Full-Blown Roses

Type: Classic Baltimore

To make this block, refer to *Volume I*, Lessons 5, 9, and 10.

With delightful informality, this block's original appears to be a symmetrical arrangement that slipped in the sewing into a relaxed asymmetry. You can see that antique block in Quilt #3 in Baltimore Album Quilts, Pattern Companion to Volume I.

The early Album scholar, Dr. William Rush Dunton, Jr., attributed the woolwork in the Baltimore-style Albums to a strong German influence (born of large German emigrations to Baltimore in mid-century). The wool stitchery is usually straight-stitching, sometimes in a scallop pattern, more often as close whip

French knots

Straight Stitch wool embroidered leaf detail

PATTERN #78: Basket of Full-Blown Roses.

Second page

stitching or discrete straight stitches rhythmically spaced around a leaf or a bud. Sometimes looped embroidery stitches were also done in the wool thread. DMC's Medici® is a marvelous wool currently available for hand-embroidery. Annie Tuley, a machine needleartist recommends a Renaissance wool thread for embroidering such a block by machine.

PATTERN #78: Basket of Full-Blown Roses.

Third page

Detail: The echoed outline
on basket, leaves, and blooms
indicates wool-whip or blanket
stitching in the original block.

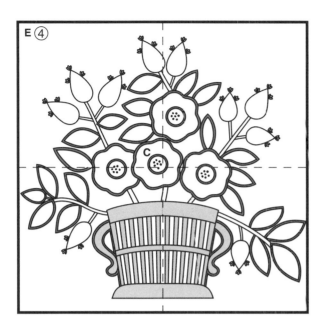

PATTERN #78: Basket of Full-Blown Roses.

Fourth page

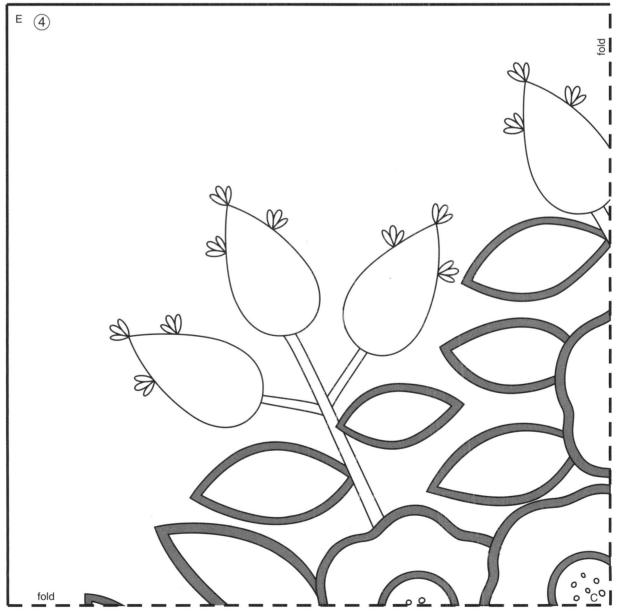

PATTERN #80: Half-Wreath of Blooms from Mrs. Mann's Quilt.

Type: Classic Baltimore

To make this block, refer in *Volume I,* to Lessons 2, 5, 9, 10.

Design a Baltimore Album Quilt! discusses all the multiple forms that wreaths take in the classic Albums. This pattern might be a half wreath, or it might simply be a stem laden to the point of falling groundward with weight. It is a repeated, though not common, block in the Albums. In Mrs. Mann's quilt (Quilt #3 in *Baltimore Album Quilts, Pattern Companion to Volume I*), the use of two of these blocks is

PATTERN #80: Half-Wreath of Blooms from Mrs. Mann's Quilt.

Second page

effective. It would be interesting to see two of these blocks adjacent and mirroring one another, or four of them arranged as a repeat block center as in Quilts #7 and #8 in *Volume I*. Quilts like #6 in *Volume I*, which frame more complex center blocks with predominantly red-and-green ones, will always welcome this kind of simple classic Album block.

PATTERN #80: Half-Wreath of Blooms from Mrs. Mann's Quilt.

Third page

PATTERN #80: Half-Wreath of Blooms from Mrs. Mann's Quilt.

Fourth page

PATTERN #82: Red Bird on a Passion Flower Branch.

Type: Baltimore-Style. (From Quilt #6 in *Dimensional Appliqué*)

To make this block, refer to Lesson 7; in *Volume I*, Lessons 5, 9, and 10.

This seems to be another block pattern by "The Whimsical Botanist's" hand in "May You, My Child, in Virtue's Path Proceed," Quilt #6 in *Dimensional Appliqué*. The tropical Passion Flower comes in purple, red, or white with touches of blue and purple. It was named by the Spaniards (who first saw it in South America) because they thought it symbolized the story of the Crucifixion. Ever since I read Dr. Dunton's reference to

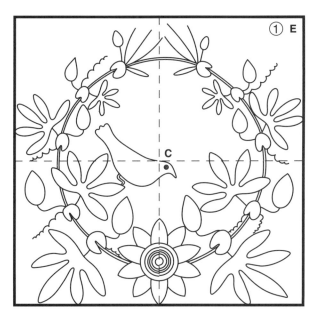

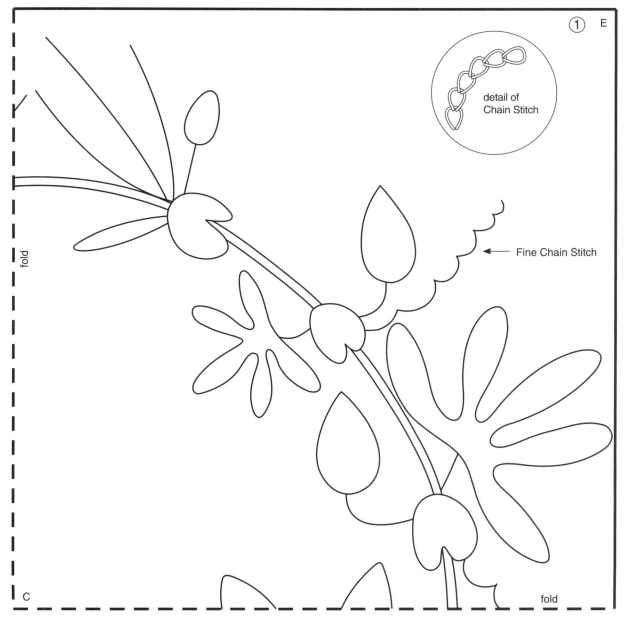

detail of Chain Stitch

Fine Chain Stitch

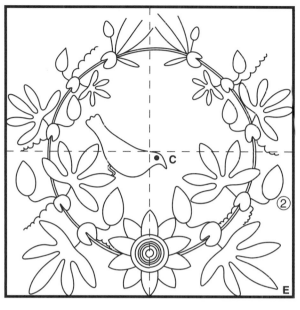

PATTERN #82: Red Bird on a Passion Flower Branch.

Second page

Passion Flowers in *Old Quilts,* this flower has intrigued me. Brenda Green kindly brought me both a fresh Passion Flower blossom from her Florida garden and this quote ("to help with the symbolism") from *Palms and Flowers of Florida:* "The fringed corona represents the halo about Christ's head, or, the crown of thorns; the pistil is for the three nails; the five stamens are five wounds; the sepals and petals stand for ten of the disciples; the young seed pod is the vinegar-soaked sponge; the tendrils are the whips; the leaves (three- or five-lobed) represent the hands of Christ."

PATTERN #82: Red Bird on a Passion Flower Branch.

Third page

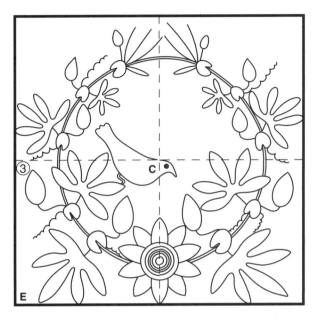

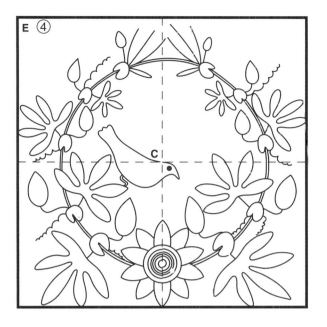

PATTERN #82: Red Bird on a Passion Flower Branch.

Fourth page

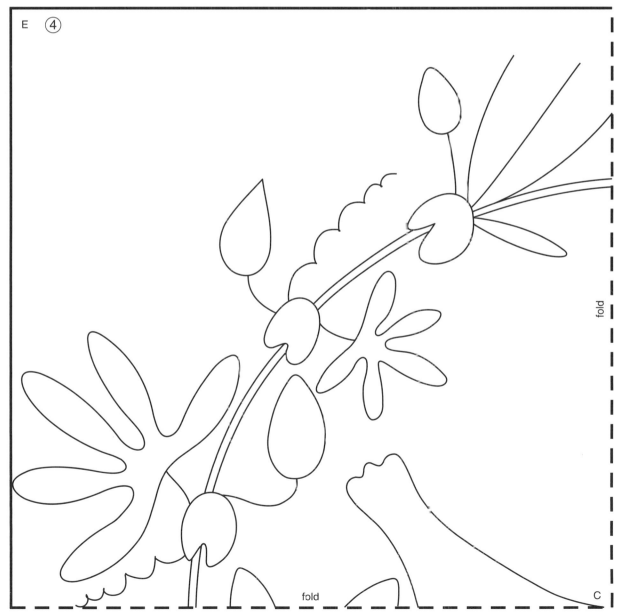

E ④

fold

fold

C

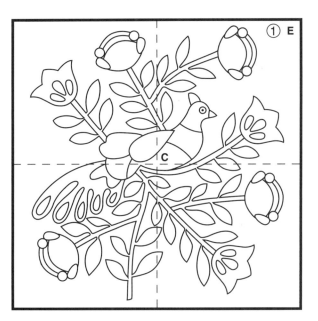

PATTERN #83: Folk Art Bird.

Type: Baltimore-Style

To make this block refer to *Volume I*, Lessons 5, 7, 9, or 10.

This graphic bird is in the style we often think of as Pennsylvania German. It is a strong, re-peated style in the Baltimore Album Quilts and may indeed reflect the German influence therein. A peacock might have been included in the Album Quilts for emblematic reasons, for it is an ancient symbol of immortality. Then, too, its tail medallions are icons for the All-Seeing Eye of God. Since the All-Seeing Eye was a prime symbol of God's omniscience

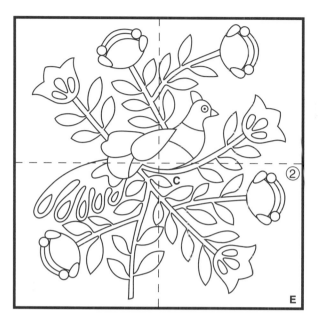

PATTERN #83: Folk Art Bird.

Second page

for both the Masons and the Odd Fellows, the peacock seems one more clear instance of intentional symbolism in the Baltimore-style Album Quilts.

PATTERN #83: Folk Art Bird.

Third page

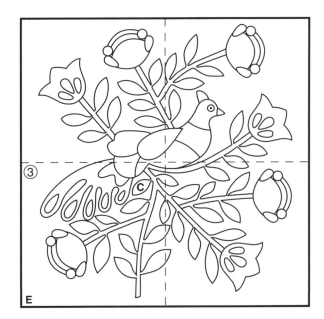

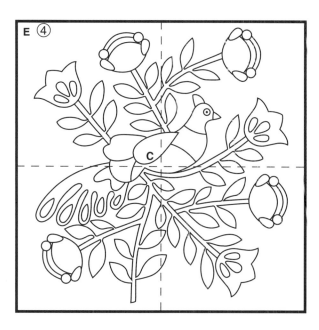

PATTERN #83: Folk Art Bird.

Fourth page

Pattern #1: "Heart Wreath of Roses"

Type: Beyond Baltimore—Author's; classically inspired

To make this block, see *Baltimore Beauties and Beyond, Vol. I*, Lessons 1 and 6

This block's antique inspiration stars in one of Lovely Lane Museum's antebellum Baltimore Album Quilts. Its symbolism is red roses for love, a heart for devotion. Such a Cutaway Appliqué block might have been cut and stitched from a solid color or a small calico print, mid-nineteenth century. Mary K. Tozer's rendition, pictured in the Color Section, typifies 20th and 21st century Baltimore Album Revival style. She has appliquéd the leaves and wreath-stem from one layer, using a large green print from the *Elly Sienkiewicz Baltimore Beauties®* designer collection for P&B Textiles. The large-scale print adds interest to the

① E   To make a full pattern:
    1. Trace the left side (top and bottom) of the pattern onto a 12½" square of freezer paper. Use a bold pen.

  2. Trace the left side onto the right side, using a light box.

Pattern #1: "Heart Wreath of Roses"

Second Page

simplicity of a cutaway design, while the cutaway method itself is particularly peaceful. Leave each calyx (bud base) open, like a pocket, to receive the buds. While the antique original had flat buds, Mary's are dimensional: Fold a 2" circle of cloth in half on the bias, right side out. Next fold it into thirds and pin. Running stitch ⅛" inside the folded circle's base. Pull the thread to gather the bud so that it fits within the calyx. Baltimore Album Revival teacher, Carol W. Jones of Anchorage, Alaska, did a series interpretation of the classic Wreathed Heart block from my first book, *Spoken Without a Word*. Carol added a berry, tulip, and acorn heart wreath. These inspired patterns 2–4 which follow.

continued on page 218

To transfer the pattern:
  1. Pin the full pattern right side up-under the green leaf-stem cloth, also right side up.
  2. Trace the leaved stem onto the green cloth for Cut-away Appliqué.
  3. Cut 24 circles, each 2" in diameter for the folded rose buds.

Pattern #2: "Heart Wreath of Acorns"

Type: Beyond Baltimore—Author's; inspired by Carol W. Jones

To make this block, see *Baltimore Beauties and Beyond, Vol. I*, Lessons 1, 9, and 11

Padded acorns were the favorite motif of Stumpwork Embroidery (15th–17th centuries). To read about the technique as applied to padded appliqué see *Fancy Appliqué*, Lesson 12, (Sienkiewicz, C&T Publishing). Next outline stitch the cap (1 strand cotton floss) and crowd it with French knots (2 strands cotton floss, 1 wrap). Mary's are opulent: "French knots (3 strands variegated floss, one wrap), 80 to 85 knots per cap!" since antiquity they have symbolized longevity, a comforting icon for an Album! By cutaway appliqué, sew the wreath-stem and acorn stems from one piece of cloth. Add the acorn/cap units as a second

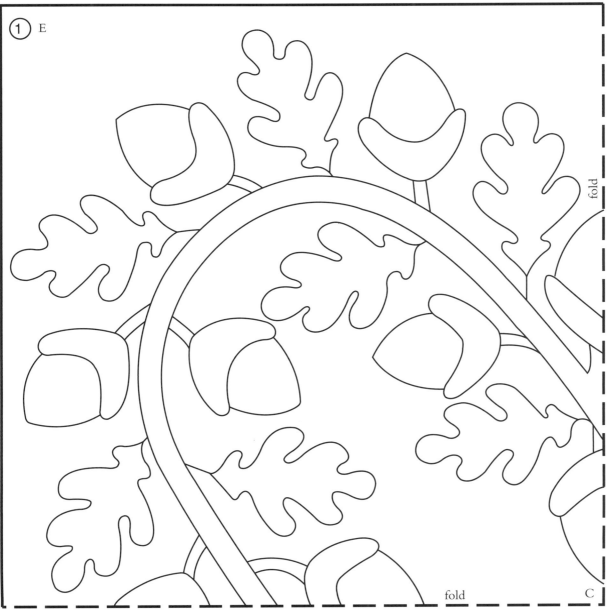

Pattern #2: "Heart Wreath of Acorns"

Second Page

layer, crowding each cap with French knots(1 strand cotton floss, two wraps) within a stem-stitched outline. Mary K. Tozer stitched this pattern's model as well as Pattern 1's. Artistically, she embroidered the leaf stems in natural gestures (1 strand cotton floss, 2-3 rows). Trace the leaf and acorn patterns onto the background cloth. Fuse the leaves or needleturn them hastily. In either case an elegant dimensionality results when next you do close blanket stitching (1 strand cotton floss) around their perimeter.Pad the acorns/ caps with a layer of thin cotton batting: trim to within 1/16" of the drawn line and glue-stick to background.

continued on page 218

Pattern #3: "Heart Wreath of Cherries"

Type: Beyond Baltimore—Author's; inspired by Carol W. Jones

To make this block, see *Baltimore Beauties and Beyond, Vol. I*, Lessons 1 and 9

I believe many different designers brought the antebellum Album Quilts to full blossom so long ago. This block may witness that process. Carol W. Jones admired my rendering of a classic Baltimore Album pattern, Wreathed Heart, in my *Spoken Without a Word* (1983). Her plays on that block's theme resulted in blocks recognizably different from the original. I, in turn, was inspired by her idea of having the heart wreath hold other symbols: grapes, acorns, tulips. I went on to draft patterns 2–4 that are recognizably different from Carol's—yet all are related to the antebellum original. Perhaps this record of design evolution within today's

Pattern #3: "Heart Wreath of Cherries"

Second Page

Baltimore Revival may help a scholar of tomorrow. Since "classic" sets a standard for all time, the Wreathed Heart has proven itself truly a classic.

Simply do this pattern's leaves, wreath-stem, and fruit stems all from one layer of cloth by Cut-way Appliqué. Or, embroider the fruit stems (1 strand each of three different color flosses, 2-3 rows, by stem or chain stitch). Make these cherries as perfect flat and stuffed circles (*Vol. 1*, Lesson 9), or as yo-yos (cut a 2" diameter circle per cherry.) If I went to the trouble of making yo-yos I'd place them gathered side up, their lovely texture for all to see!

continued on page 218

Pattern #4: "Heart Wreath of Tulips"

Type: Beyond Baltimore—Author's; inspired by Carol W. Jones

To make this block, see *Baltimore Beauties and Beyond, Vol. I*, Lessons 1, 5 and 6

Like this book's Heart Wreath of Cherries and Heart Wreath of Acorns, this block was inspired by Carol W. Jones's block that was in turn inspired by a classic block pattern called "The $100,000 Tulips" in *Baltimore Beauties and Beyond, Vol. I*. That block's name celebrated the first antique Baltimore-style Album Quilt to sell for over $100,000. It sold at Sotheby's Auction House, NYC, in January, 1987.

This block's flowers invite some fabric folding. A fan-like pleated flower seems a simple possibility. I've also wondered about having the center tulip petal made

fold

E ①

C   fold

Pattern #4: "Heart Wreath of Tulips"

Second Page

from a folded circle; or even all three petals. If you find the answer I'd love to see it! Used together and repeated (see page 119, "Heart-Garlanded Album", in the Color Section) these blocks can be a powerful unifier in a classic Album Quilt's set. The four hearts, placed on the diagonal, would also make graphic corner blocks, pointing to a quilt's center.

Needleartist Note: This block's model, pictured in the Color Section, was interpreted and made by Arden Macy in 2001. She writes, "I am a mother of two and grandmother of five. By profession I'm a registered medical technologist. Though fairly new at quilting, I am realizing I've always wanted to make a Baltimore Album Quilt!"

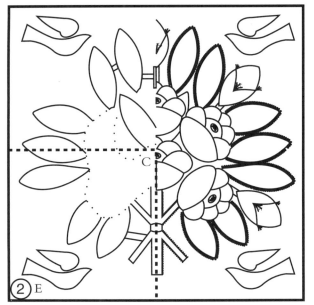

Pattern #5: "Baltimore Rose Bouquet"

Type: Beyond Baltimore—Author's interpretation of a classic style

To make this block, see *Baltimore Beauties and Beyond, Vol. I*, Lessons 1, 5, and 7

This simple bouquet is dramatic even when unembellished. Lesson 5 of *Vol. I* explains the temporary "pattern bridge" concept. The left half of this pattern shows you the pattern-bridged Foliage Layout. Cut it out (leaving the bridges attached) double-on-the-fold. Pattern bridges allow you to transfer an interrupted pattern (one in which not all the pieces of one color touch each other) as a single paper doily-like freezer paper pattern. In this block, cut the bridged foliage pattern (the leaves, calyxes, and stems) from a sheet of freezer paper and iron this single cut-out to a 13"

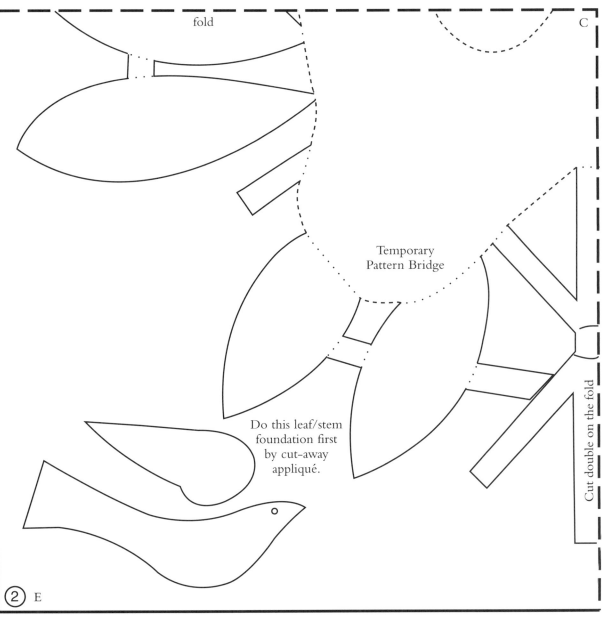

fold

C

Temporary
Pattern Bridge

Do this leaf/stem
foundation first
by cut-away
appliqué.

Cut double on the fold

② E

Pattern #5: "Baltimore Rose Bouquet"

Second Page

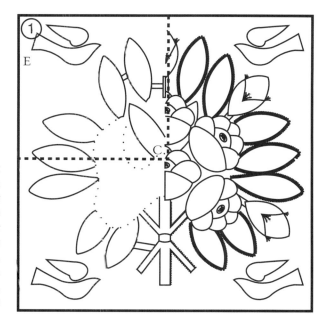

square of green cloth. Cut and sew the appliquéd foliage a little bit at a time by Cutaway Appliqué. Iron the finished foliage appliqué from the back, working over a worn terry cloth towel. Use spray starch and a paper towel press cloth if desired.

Next, add the roses, buds, and birds by separate unit appliqué. Working over a lightbox, I'd draw them in pencil or Pigma pen onto the background cloth. For such simple shapes I'd draw the exact pattern line. The appliqué can be done by needleturn with freezer paper on top. Use the pin-placement method to make sure the paper shape is directly above the drawn shape, then baste the appliqué in place. To do *Vol. I*, Lesson 10's prepared appliqué with freezer paper inside, simply prepare each shape and baste it right over the

The Foliage Layout Pattern is linked by temporary pattern bridges. Trace the foliage only onto freezer paper and iron, centered, onto the right side up of the 12 ½" square of green cloth.

Pattern #5: "Baltimore Rose Bouquet"

Third Page

drawn line. Stitching in and out of the drawn line, in and out of the fold, guarantees you'll cover your placement lines.

Stuffed roses: Cut the pattern shape out of 3 layers of thin, dense cotton batting. Thinking of these as stacked layers like a wedding cake. Trim each layer (including the base layer) so that it is 1/16" smaller than the one below it. Glue-stick the layers together, as with frosting between cake layers. Now turn the stack like an upside down wedding cake and glue-stick it smallest layer first, to the background. Iron a freezer paper rose template to the right side of the appliqué cloth and cut the seam a full 1/2" wide so that (after basting and during needle-turn) it tucks comfortably under the padding, without distorting the background.

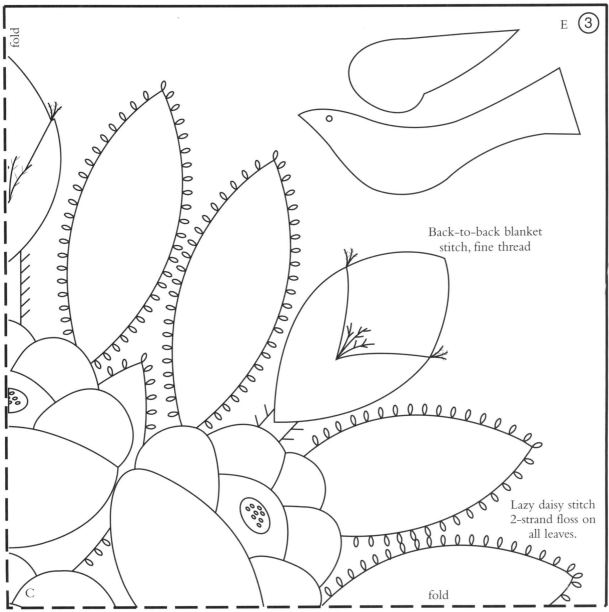

Back-to-back blanket stitch, fine thread

Lazy daisy stitch 2-strand floss on all leaves.

fold

Pattern #5: "Baltimore Rose Bouquet"

Fourth Page

After appliquéing, big-stitch quilt the petals through the batting layers. Embroider (1-2 strands, cotton floss, stem or chain stitch) the rose's outline and over the quilted lines around its petals. This heavy padding under an embroidered cover is what I've taught as Stumpwork Appliqué in Lesson 12 of *Fancy Appliqué*. The Color Section shows two versions of this pattern.

Needleartist Note: Patty Henry made one version in 2001 and writes, "As a cloth artist, I have been able to express my personal thoughts, feelings, and beliefs, using fabric and embellishments. My passion incorporates techniques learned in childhood: appliqué, embroidery, and beading." The second model was made in 2002 by Cynthia Williford, whose Needleartist Note appears with Pattern 7.

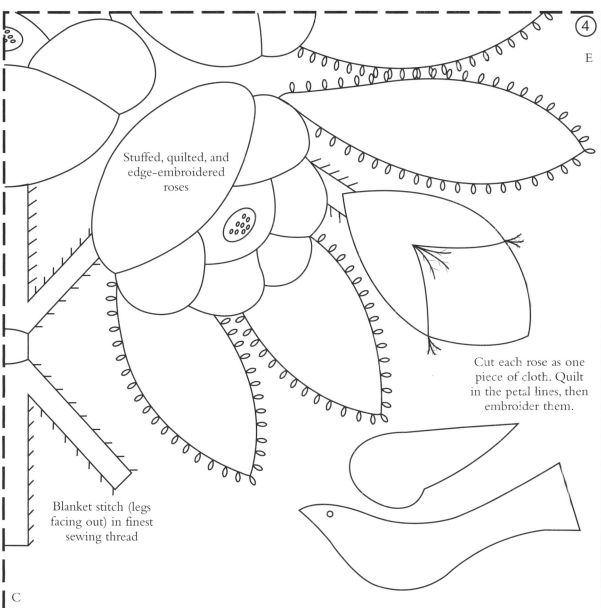

Stuffed, quilted, and edge-embroidered roses

Cut each rose as one piece of cloth. Quilt in the petal lines, then embroider them.

Blanket stitch (legs facing out) in finest sewing thread

② E

Pattern #6: "Baltimore Basket of Roses"

Type: Beyond Baltimore—Author's; interpretation of a classic style

To make this block, see *Baltimore Beauties and Beyond, Vol. I*, Lessons 1 and 10

Patterns 5, 6, and 7 all invite padded and embroidered appliqué, an antique Baltimore style whose exploration beckons even those who have long been on this Album journey. Trace Pattern 6, double on the fold, so that you get the full pattern. The padding and embroidery notes for Pattern 5 can usefully be re-read in relation to this block. This pattern's foliage could be done by Cutaway with a pattern-bridged template made in the same way as that of Pattern 5. Or, it could be done by separate-unit appliqué using freezer paper inside or on top. The fact that the same leaf is repeated nine times also makes this block ideal for prepared appliqué using freezer paper inside.

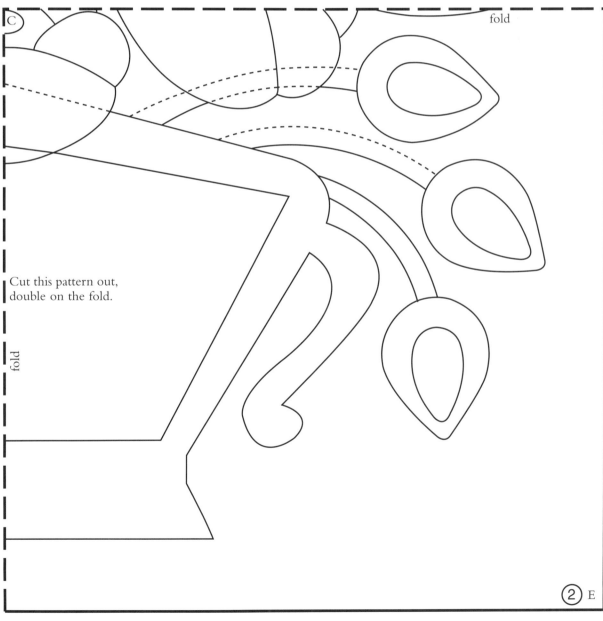

C

fold

Cut this pattern out, double on the fold.

fold

② E

Pattern #6: "Baltimore Basket of Roses"

Second Page

This is a popular technique that is taught, if you are not already familiar with it, in Lesson 10, *Vol. I*. To do the bud stems by the superfine stem method (*Vol. I*, Lesson 9), mark only their dotted pattern line on the background line.

The basket's center can be reverse appliquéd or simply appliquéd and invites a jazzy print, a plaid, or even slender basket reeds. Play at darkening the morning glories' throats. They could be emphasized with some darker colored embroidery and a cluster of French knots at the center, perhaps? Enjoy!

continued on page 218

Pattern #7: "Baltimore Urn of Roses"

Type: Beyond Baltimore—Author's, classically inspired

To make this block, see *Baltimore Beauties and Beyond, Vol. I,* Lessons 1, 5, and 7

Cynthia Williford added the urn's sash and oval medallion. She shares, "For the embroidery on the vase and flowers, I used silk floss from the Thread Gatherer (TG): Frosted Auburn for the reds, Yellow Blush for the yellows and peach tones; Wild Violets for the light greens, blues, and violets; and Desert Dawn for the pinks. For the medium and dark greens on both the vase and the appliqué leaves, I used Au Ver à Soie (silk) floss. I used a dark green and a medium green (color 3424). For the stitches, I used bullions, French knots, lazy daisy, and buttonhole. I used one strand of floss, except on the center roses where I used two strands.

Pattern #7: "Baltimore Urn of Roses"

Second Page

The small French knots around the center roses (in yellow) are one stand, one wrap; the rest of the French knots are one strand, three wraps. The bullions inside petals are 8 or 9 wraps and build up to 14. I couched the lace on the vase with chain stitched Kreinik Metallics Fine Braid #8, color 002.

Needleartist Note: Cynthia Williford writes, "From my mother, who sews meticulously, and the dear Irish nuns, who taught me to do handwork, I was convinced early on I was born with a needle in my hand. Now, as a homeschooling mother of six boys, hand sewing is my quiet refuge."

continued on page 218

Pattern #8: "Squared Wreath of Embroidered Flowers"

Type: Beyond Baltimore—Author's; classically inspired

To make this block, see *Baltimore Beauties and Beyond, Vol. I*, Lessons 1, 9, and 10

This block's asymmetrical archetype is richly embroidered. Pale green straight stitch edges leaves and stems. Pink satin-stitched petals surround a red cloth center. Begin by making this simplified Master Pattern: Trace the quadrant below, clockwise, onto a 12 ½" paper square. Place the wreath stem's bias, raw edges on the dashed line (*Vol. I*, Lesson 9). For Lesson 10's prepared appliqué with freezer paper inside, cut leaf templates in the A, B, C, and D sizes. Embroider the flower stems (two strands, cotton floss, close rows of stem or chain stitch).

continued on page 218

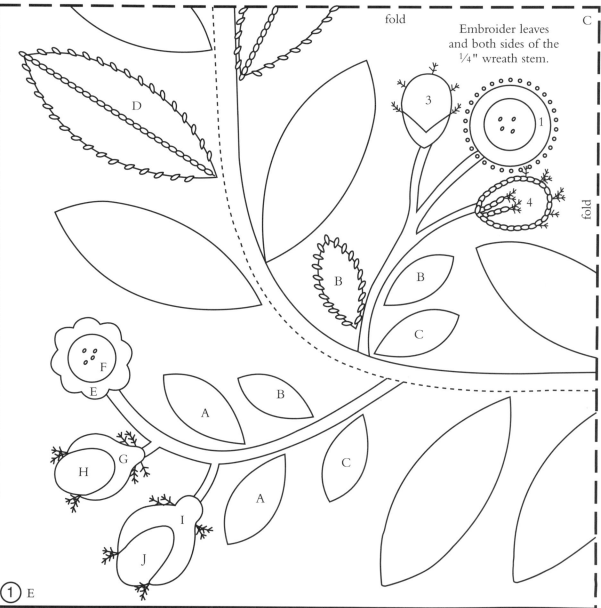

Embroider leaves and both sides of the ¼" wreath stem.

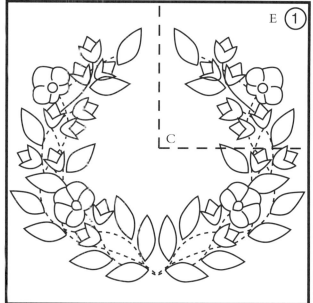

Pattern #9: "Intertwined Crown of Flowers" The Stem Layout

Type: Beyond Baltimore—Author's, classically inspired.

To make this block, see *Baltimore Beauties and Beyond, Vol. I*, Lessons 1, 5, 9, and 10

In this elegant red and green study, red buds and roses and green leaves emanate from intertwined stems. First trace one half of The Stem Pattern, then the other half to make a Master Layout. Trace the six different stem paths onto the background cloth, beginning or ending under a leaf or bud. Make stem #1-5 either with commercial bias bars (3/16"), or by *Vol. 1*, Lesson 9's superfine stem method. Marjorie Mahoney suggests cutting about 80" of 5/8"-wide bias strips, folding and basting in thirds, then basting to the marked background, one at a time. Embroider stem

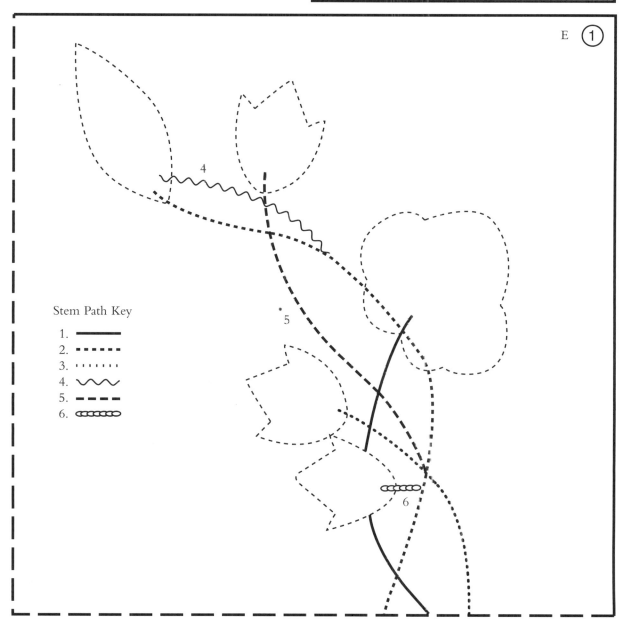

Stem Path Key

1. ──────
2. ▪▪▪▪▪▪
3. ⋯⋯⋯⋯
4. ∿∿∿∿
5. ▬ ▬ ▬ ▬
6. ⬤⬤⬤⬤⬤

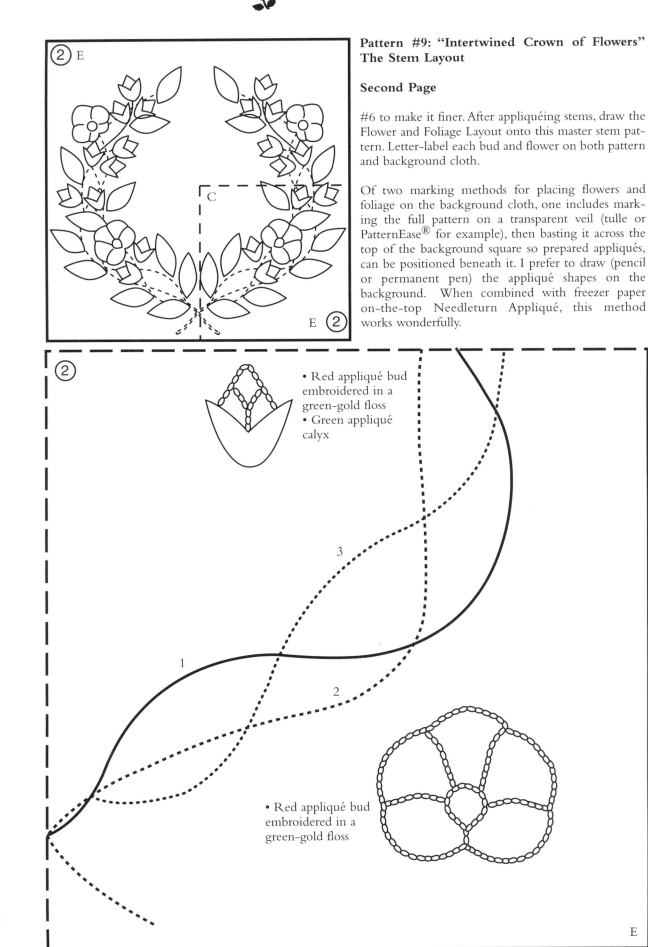

Pattern #9: "Intertwined Crown of Flowers" The Stem Layout

Second Page

#6 to make it finer. After appliquéing stems, draw the Flower and Foliage Layout onto this master stem pattern. Letter-label each bud and flower on both pattern and background cloth.

Of two marking methods for placing flowers and foliage on the background cloth, one includes marking the full pattern on a transparent veil (tulle or PatternEase® for example), then basting it across the top of the background square so prepared appliqués, can be positioned beneath it. I prefer to draw (pencil or permanent pen) the appliqué shapes on the background. When combined with freezer paper on-the-top Needleturn Appliqué, this method works wonderfully.

• Red appliqué bud embroidered in a green-gold floss
• Green appliqué calyx

• Red appliqué bud embroidered in a green-gold floss

Pattern #9: "Intertwined Crown of Flowers"

Third Page

Once the stems are appliquéd, leaves, buds and roses follow. The leaves use three templates, (A, B, C) and could be needleturned, or prepared with freezer paper inside (*Vol I.*, Lesson 10), or on top (Lessons 2 and 5). Pad the buds with one layer of batting or make them from 1 ½"-diameter folded cloth circles, folded in half, then in thirds. Pad the roses with up to three layers of batting (see Pattern 5). Use ½" seam allowance so the appliqué's loft rises above but does not distort the background. Pin-place roses, freezer paper on top, then baste in place. Needleturn, stitching the appliqué's seam line by going in and out of the drawn line, then up to catch the fold to stitch the padded rose onto the marked background.

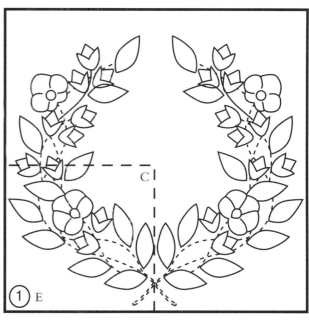

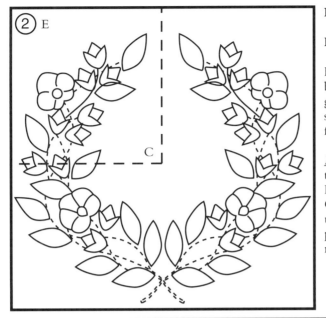

Pattern #9: "Intertwined Crown of Flowers"

Fourth Page

Finish by big-stitch-quilting the embroidery lines on buds and roses, then embroidering (2 strands green/gold or moss green cotton chainstitch) stem stitch over the quilting lines and around each flower's edge.

Needleartist Note: Nancy Kerns, a beloved (NQA certified) teacher of quiltmaking in New Jersey's Pennington area, has completed two Baltimore Album Quilts, one a reproduction of an antique Album attributed to Mary Mannakee. The other, which took a first place in the 2001 NJ State Quilt Guild Show, is a record of Nancy's own Album journey.

Pattern #10: "Theorem-Style Urn of Fruit"

Type: Classic Baltimore, from a quilt in Baltimore's Numsen family

To make this block, see *Baltimore Beauties and Beyond, Vol. I,* Lessons 1 and 10.

In *Papercuts and Plenty, Vol. III of Baltimore Beauties and Beyond,* I explored oil stencil–shading of cloth, in the manner of eighteenth and nineteenth century theorem paintings. Recently, in making this book's cover block, I realized an old dream—to imitate the glowingly antique fabric of the original block's urn (pictured in that now out-of-print volume). It was done by stenciling multiple colors (but primarily Prussian blue) onto the monochromatic taupe print urn cloth. The chevron design was created with masking tape to darken first one side (directing the color layers), then the other, creating a mountain peak effect. I was

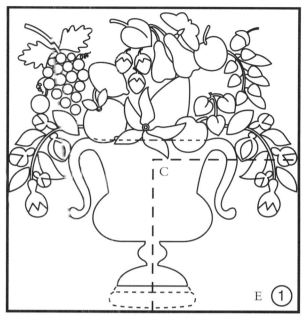

Pattern #10: "Theorem-Style Urn of Fruit"

Second Page

pleased as well by the dimensional look of the fruit; the colored prints were darkened to roundness by oil pastel stenciling. To try oil pastel shading yourself, make a window template for each appliqué shape: First draw the shape (an apple, for example), then cut it out of freezer paper (or self-stick paper) 2" larger all around than the shape itself. Finally, cut the appliqué shape from the center. This remaining frame is the "window" used for stenciling. Iron the window template onto the right side of the appliqué fabric. Stabilize the cloth with another piece of freezer paper ironed shiny side to the fabric's wrong side. Scribble pastel colors onto the window frame. To make a pastel "finger brush," cover your forefinger with a muslin cloth and push the pastel off the frame, onto the cloth beneath. Each time you push across

Pattern #10: "Theorem-Style Urn of Fruit"

Third Page

the frame (of an apple cut-out, say) the shading will darken the apple's outline and shade softly toward its center.

Oil pastels with the most oil in them work best. (Oil paintsticks work extremely well but are more expensive yet.) The more oil, the more pigment. The best are top artist quality (Sakura Specialist Craypas® for example.) From testing, the less high quality (less expensive) oil pastels are less intense and fade a bit with washing, but do not run. You may want to try less expensive ones first, then invest in the largest box (36-50 colors) you can afford. For fruit, darken the outside of each shape, leaving the area lightest where a light source would strike. It is easier and more successful to darken a fabric than to add white highlights.

Pattern #10: "Theorem–Style Urn of Fruit"

Fourth Page

Heat-set the oil pastels using a tissue as a presscloth. This sets the color and can be done within an hour of coloring. The result is gently washable.

Techniques from *Fancy Appliqué* are used: inking, embroidery, UltraSuede® appliqué, and ribbon appliqué. This block's antique original was appliquéd out of cotton prints, so the theorem appliqué (the oil stencil shading) is my *Beyond Baltimore* interpretation. At the time of this book's publication, the Elly Sienkiewicz Baltimore Beauties® III for P & B Textiles fabric line is current. The cover block's cotton appliqués are all from that fabric line. The background is one of the Baltimore Beauties® printed style backgrounds I now prefer for Album blocks, #866 E, but the urn and pears are hard to recognize as the neutral

continued on page 218

Pattern #11: "Grape-Flanked Urn of Fruit"

Type: Classic Baltimore

To make this block, see *Baltimore Beauties and Beyond, Vol. I*, Lessons 1 and 10

I had drawn this pattern from a quilt originating in Baltimore's Numsen family a decade or more ago, but never made it. The levitating look of the fruit charmed me, but I had kept no color reference to go with the pattern. At the Maryland Historical Society's 2001 show and in their magnificent catalogue, *The Baltimore Album Quilt Tradition*, I saw pictured a

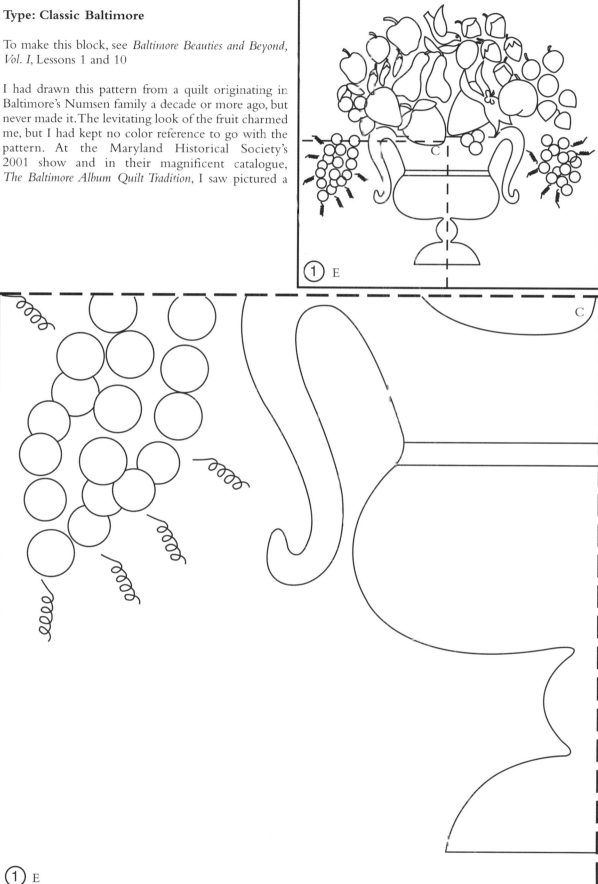

Pattern #11: "Grape-Flanked Urn of Fruit"

Second Page

similar block in an 1848 quilt belonging to the Lovely Lane Museum and made by the Ladies of the Greene Street Methodist Church in Baltimore. This block is very similar to Pattern 10 (even the same urn fabric was used in both the Lovely Lane quilt and the Numsen family quilt). Such a complex block invites a color lesson: How does one go about choosing the fabric for a block with many appliqués? A simple way to do it is to identify the basic colors: three yellow fruits, two blue fruits, four red fruits, pink urn, for example. Then you need to choose fabrics in these color groups. In antique Baltimores, two blues were often the same blue, for less variety was used within one block. We moderns, however, can

Pattern #11: "Grape-Flanked Urn of Fruit"

Third Page

stick to simplicity or follow our fancy. Cutting 3" swatches and pinning them to your background cloth will give you a good start. Your greens can happily mix blue-greens and yellow-greens or stick to one family of greens if you prefer.

Today, several times a year, fabric designers come out with multiple "collections" designed to mix well with one another. The cover block was all made from an Elly Sienkiewicz Baltimore Beauties® for P & B Textiles collection which made it easier to choose my reds, yellows, blues, and greens. Lynn Thurston began this block with that collection but then added her own choices to it. Whether by interesting print use or

Pattern #11: "Grape-Flanked Urn of Fruit"

Fourth Page

embellishment with thread, beads, ribbon, or paint, these urns are invitations to display your appliqué artistry!

Needleartist Note: Previously published for original designs in macramé and counted-cross stitch, Lynn became interested in quilting in the early 1990s. She prefers to work on a small scale in her piecing and appliqué, but has undertaken a queen-size Baltimore Album project.

Pattern #12: "Theorem-Style Urn of Flowers"

Type: Beyond Baltimore, drawn by the author

To make this block, see *Baltimore Beauties and Beyond, Vol. I*, Lessons 1, 9, and 10

This pattern interprets an antique Baltimore urn made of the same cloth I sought (with oil pastels) to imitate on the front cover block. Though not as flower-filled as the original bouquet, it is a rich example of the ornate, skillfully drawn design for which Baltimore became famous. I designed the floral outline specifically to fill the Baltimore Beauties® 12½" design image area in a more pleasing way than the original. This square could be made by flat appliqué or

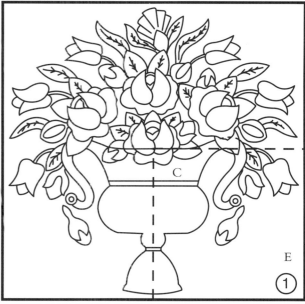

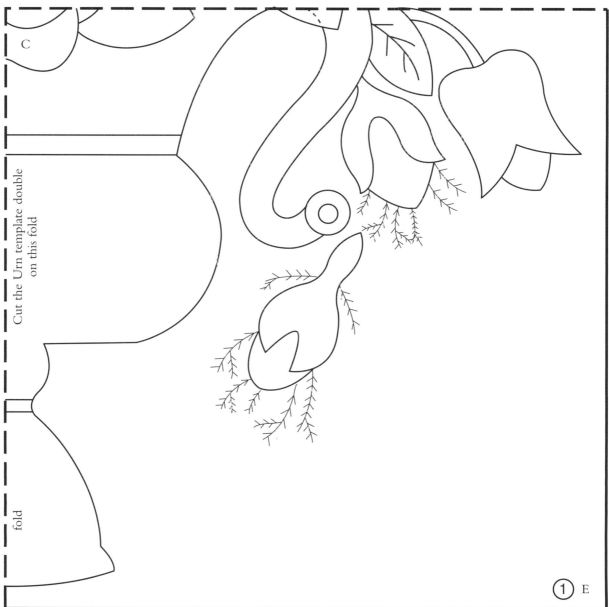

Cut the Urn template double on this fold

fold

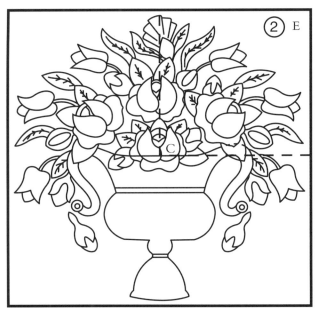

Pattern #12: "Theorem-Style Urn of Flowers"

Second Page

skillfully padded. (*Fancy Appliqué's* Lesson 12 is applicable, showing how to pad with scaled-back layers of thin batting.) This block sings when, as Bette Augustine has done, it is made of carefully chosen prints and solids. It also invites the sort of oil paintstick or pastel stencil shading taught in *Papercuts and Plenty* and reviewed in Pattern 11's notes. Making this pattern is a masterful accomplishment, so it makes a fitting finale to this compendium of designs.

Source Note: For Theorem-Stenciled Appliqué, Sakura Specialist Oil Pastels can be ordered from Dick Blick 1-800-447-8192. For a quiltshop or mail order supplier carrying Elly Sienkiewicz's Baltimore Beauties® for P&B Textiles call P&B at 1-800-TLC-BEAR.

Pattern #12: "Theorem-Style Urn of Flowers"

Third Page

<u>Needleartist Note:</u> The elegant model pictured was made by Bette Florette Augustine who writes, "The colors of fabric, ribbon, and thread mixed with the lure of unlimited appliqué design possibilities have been pulling me toward Baltimore-style blocks for years. Beginning with the mysteries of my grandmother's button box, I have been guided to a time in my life where I can not only stitch my own Baltimore-inspired blocks, but also help others find their place in the history of needlewomen through my affiliation [as Director] with The Elly Sienkiewicz Appliqué Academy. I am truly blessed!"

Pattern #12: "Theorem-Style Urn of Flowers

Fourth Page

Patterns (continued)

Pattern #1, continued from page 19

the times you can, To all the people you can, As long as ever you can." This injunction from the founder of the Methodism appeals both because of its sentiment and because it serves as a memorial to the Methodist influence in the Baltimore Album Quilts.

Dr. Dunton, in *Old Quilts*, points out the strong Methodist hand in many, though not all, of these quilts. Numerous names from these Baltimore quilts are recorded in mid-nineteenth-century Methodist class lists and in family genealogies connected to these quilts. Quilts were often inscribed to Methodist class leaders and ministers and there are even picture blocks of churches.

Brought to the United States in the 1760s, Methodism first took root in New York, New Jersey, Pennsylvania, and Maryland. The Church in America followed founder John Wesley's precept of people gathered into classes for Christian fellowship under the guidance of a lay leader. Several points seem pertinent to the Album Quilts. First, the weekly class system meant that while one attended one's regular class weekly, on a given Sunday a Baltimorean might attend any Methodist church in the Baltimore Conference. This institutionalized mixing of great numbers of Methodists might help explain how particular quilt sets and block patterns, fabrics, and styles in the Baltimore Album Quilts could be spread within the church and community as a whole on such a scale.

Second, Methodism in the mid-nineteenth century had a heightened social conscience expressed by communal concern over social evils, "sweated labor, poverty, and squalor." The Album Quilts would surely reflect some of these concerns. From its beginning, American Methodism had a missionary purpose as well and sent its first missionaries to Africa in 1833, to South America in 1835, and to China in 1847. In *Old Quilts* (p. 153), Dr. Dunton notes three missionary-connected repeat block Album Quilts, though the denomination they represent is uncertain. One, of repeated fleurs-de-lis, is inscribed, in part, "Presented to Rev. Mr. Minor by/the Young Ladies of/Thorndale Seminary./The names of the contributors being written on the quilt." Another square reads "Rev. Mr. Minor of the African Mission."

The Baltimore Albums may signal pro- or anti-slavery sympathies by the presence or absence of the "Phrygian" or "freedom" cap in the eagle blocks. In that context, it's interesting to note that Maryland was a slaveholding state, whose citizens were severely divided on the issue. After the 1844 General Conference opened the way for a pro-slavery Methodist Episcopal Church South, the Baltimore Conference joined the Northern, anti-slavery, Methodist churches. Yet more insight into who made these quilts might possibly be gathered through studying *The Ladies Repository and Gathering of the West*, a women's literary magazine from the Methodist publishing house.

The Methodist emphasis on a life guided by love was fervently espoused as well by fraternal orders, including the Masons and the Odd Fellows, whose symbols seem so pervasive in these quilts (and a topic discussed in detail in Volume II). From whatever sources, the very ethos of fellowship and love, love of God, love of Country, love of friends, pervades the Album Quilts.

Pattern #6, continued from page 23

As a Victorian man of letters, Andersen would have understood the symbol's meanings – hearts speak of Love, Devotion, or Charity. And as for the swans in this pattern? They are my addition and symbolize Andersen's fairy tale, "The Ugly Duckling."

Pattern #8, continued from page 25

Baltimore, during the three decades before the Civil War, was the port of entry for thousands of German immigrants. Though some earned passage for the return journey aboard Baltimore's cotton and tobacco exporting boats, many stayed. Because a strong Methodist connection to the Baltimore Albums is well documented, it is noteworthy that certain of Baltimore's Methodist churches were essentially German churches.

Pattern #11, continued from page 27

Most classic and neoclassic representations of the acanthus leaf are more curvacious. This angular version looks at least equally close to the botanical original.

Pattern #15, continued from page 29

The grape may be the most common fruit in the largely Christian Baltimore Album Quilts. Grapes symbolize Christ's Blood in the Eucharist, while wild grapes symbolizes Charity. Christ is referred to as the True Vine.

Pattern #18, continued from page 31

Authors note: Research spearheaded by Jennifer Goldsborough highlights the fact that the Maryland Institution for the Promotion of the Mechanic Arts held annual fairs in Baltimore at which Albums were exhibited 1848-1856. Newspapers in the Collection of the Maryland Historical Society document that the quilts were judged and that one year's winner might become a judge the next year.

Pattern #9, continued from page 54

Note: The secret to easy Reverse Applique is a fine (not heavy) threaded background cloth and curved (not pointed) bases on the feathers. P&B Textile's Elly Sienkiewicz/Baltimore Beauties® line works well.

Pattern #12, continued from page 56

and it is intended also to refer to the spirit in which those acts are to be performed" (*Odd Fellows Monitor and Guide*, p. 47). And do these not seem appropriate symbols for family precepts as well?

Patterns (continued)

Pattern #7, continued from page 77

Rick Rack Roses: The diameter of the finished flower can be varied both by the width of the rick rack used and by the length of the strip used.

1. Braiding rick rack: Hold the length of rick rack folded in half in your left hand. With your right hand, wind one half of the strip in front of, then behind, the other strip which is stationary. Repeat this "braiding" so the points of one strip link into the valleys of the other (see illustration).

2. Next, roll this braided strip four times around the folded end where you started. Wrap tightly to form the rose's center petals. The bottom will be flat with all the points at one level. Sew this base by whip-stitching one row to another with red thread. For this large rose, continue wrapping and whipstitching until the unused braid is about 10" long. Secure the last stitches.

3. Now sew gathering stitches (one in and out of each point) at the inner edge of the strip. Pull thread to gather gently and wind this strip around the bud base's outer ridge, forming its more open outer petals.

4. Overcast the outer petal points to the bud base. Tuck under the raw-edged end so it is hidden under the flower. Secure your last stitches. If there is any excess length of braid, trim it off to adjust the flower's size.

Pattern #1, continued from page 185

Needleartist Note: Mary K. Tozer stitched this model in 2001. She writes, "I have been making quilts since 1990 and doing appliqué and embroidery since 1998. My life's motto: Dance as if no one were watching; Sing as if no one were listening."

Pattern #2, continued from page 187

Optionally, cut the acorn/cap appliqué as one unit, leaving a full ¼" seam allowance to tuck under the batting. Appliqué in and out of the drawn line (to cover it), and come up to catch the appliqué's turnline fold. This block's model was lost in a workshop Elly taught. If you have any information, please contact Elly through C&T Publishing.

Pattern # 3, continued from page 189

Needleartist Note: Melinda K. Hiles made this model. She writes, "As a child, I was inspired by the needlework of both my grandmothers and by my mother's contagious enthusiasm for quilting. I have been quilting for five years and I recently finished my first completely hand-sewn quilt."

Pattern #6, continued from page 197

Needleartist Note: Jayne Slovick stitched this block's exuberant model. As a beginning quilter she lived in Pennsylvania, where quilting inspiration, exposure, and education abounds. Now living in Idaho, she is a quiltmaking instructor with a special focus on Baltimore Album Quilts.

Pattern #7, continued from page 199

Source Note: *The Thread Gatherer,* 2108 Norcrest, Boise, ID 83705. I used this also for the French knots on the lace (one strand, one wrap) and for the vase bottom chain stitch. I couched 4mm silk ribbon (TG Desert Dawn) down with French knots (TG Desert Dawn silk floss, one strand, three wraps) at the center and toward the bottom. Then I outline stitched the edge using one strand of medium green silk. The bumblebees' underwing is antique lace; their upper wing, modern lace. Their legs are couched down chenille thread. Their eyes are four mixed beads each, Mill Hill number's 3036 and 3026."

Pattern #8, continued from page 200

Choose one style flower (#1 or 2) and bud (#3 or 4) and repeat it throughout.

Needleartist Note: Marjorie Mahoney made this block's model and writes, "I began quilting in 1960 and 30 years later, in 1990, I discovered Baltimore Album Appliqué. Now, my life at 80 years is a joy to live, knowing the pleasure of stitching each day, yet another beautiful Baltimore Album block."

Pattern #10, continued from page 208

feather print #860U. Like the antique original, you can simply choose shaded fabric and evocative prints to enhance the block's artistry. As I write this, my friend and teaching colleague, Anne Connery, has done this same block all in cotton appliqué, but with such exquisite fabric selection that it sings. This block's model was made in 2000 by Elly Sienkiewicz.

Source Note: The Sakura Specialist Oil Pastels can be ordered from your local art supply or from Dick Blick (1-800-447-8192). P&B Textile's office number is 1-800-TLC-BEAR to inquire where Elly's Baltimore Beauties line is sold near you or by mail.

Index to the *Baltimore Beauties* series Patterns and Techniques

Key to books listed in the Index. Book abbreviations are followed by the page number. Patterns included in this volume are preceded by a star (★).

AP12 =Appliqué 12 Easy Ways!

BorMed =Appliqué 12 Borders 7 Medallions

BAQ = Baltimore Album Quilts, the Pattern Companion to Baltimore Beauties and Beyond, Volume 1

BAR = Baltimore Album Revival!

DA = Dimensional Appliqué

DABAQ =Design a Baltimore Album Quilt!

SWAW = Spoken Without a Word

Vol. I =Baltimore Beauties and Beyond, Volume 1

Vol. II = Baltimore Beauties and Beyond, Volume 2

Vol. III = Papercuts and Plenty, Baltimore Beauties and Beyond, Volume 3

BOB = The Best of Baltimore Beauties

BOB II = The Best of Baltimore Beauties II

Key to type of pattern:

B = "Beyond" Baltimore, a quilt or block pattern beyond Baltimore in time or space

C = Classic Baltimore, a quilt or block pattern taken from a Baltimore Album quilt of the 19th century

P = Papercut or "Snowflake" pattern

S = Baltimore-style pattern, a quilt or block pattern that looks like a mid-19th century quilt but has uncertain provenance

T = Traditional Appliqué pattern (not Baltimore-Style), whether antique or contemporary

THE PATTERNS

★Abstract Design, B, P, *Vol. III*, 104, *BOB II,* 128

★Abstract Design II, B, P, *Vol. III*, 108, *BOB II,* 130

Acanthus Leaves with Hearts and Arrow, C, *SWAW*, 30

Acorn and Oak Leaf Frame, B, P, *Vol. II*, 117, *BOB*, 108

Albertine's Rose Climber, B, *BAQ*, 84

Album, The, C, *BAQ*, 128, *BOB*, 69

Album Block Case, *Vol. III*, 198

★Album in a Rose Lyre Wreath, C, *Vol. III*, 150, *BOB II*, 161

★Alex's Cats (from *Classic Revival: Alex's Album*), B, P, *Vol. III*, 112, *BOB II*, 133

Angular Rose Vine Border, *DA*, Pullout

★Annie Tuley's Pleated Basket, B, *DA*, 161, *BOB II*, 110

★Apples in the Late Afternoon, B, *DA*, 120, *BOB II*, 90

Asymmetrical Spray of Red Blossoms I, C, *BAQ*, 76, *BOB*, 47

★Baltimore Basket of Roses, B, *BOB II*, 196

★Baltimore Bouquet, B, *DA*, 144, *BOB II*, 102

★Baltimore Rose Bouquet, B, *BOB II*, 192

★Baltimore Urn of Roses, B, *BOB II*, 198

Basic Basket with Berried Foliage Base and Brim, B, *DA*, 162, *BOB*, 163

Basic Basket with Linked-Circles, Base and Brim, B, *DA*, 162, *BOB*, 163

Basic Basket with Braided Base and Brim, B, *DA*, 162, *BOB*, 163

★Basket of Full-Blown Roses, C, *Vol. III*, 161, *BOB II*, 168

★Basket of Quarter Roses and Buds, B, *DA*, 108, *BOB II*, 82

Basket of Flowers Pattern, *BOB*, 211

Basket with Blooms, Bird and Bible (medallion), C, *SWAW*, 32; see also Updegraf

Be My Valentine (quilt), T, *AP12*, 14

Beribboned Feather Border, C, *BorMed*, 27

Beribboned Irish Chain (quilt), T, *AP12*, 76

★Betty Alderman's *Scherenschnitte*, B, P, *BAQ*, 21, *BOB II*, 21

Bird Bedecked Bouquet, S, *BAQ*, 70, *BOB*, 41

★Bird in a Fruit Wreath, C, *Vol. II*, 128, *BOB II*, 58

Bonnie's Hearts and Angels Border, B, *BorMed*, 16

Botanical Variation (from *Classic Revival: Alex's Album*), C, P, *Vol. III*, 114

Botanical Variation (from *Classic Revival: Alex's Album*, three patterns), S, P, *Vol. III*, 111, 124, 125, *BOB*, 170

Botanical Variation in Honor of Victoria Jean McKibben Hamilton (from *Classic Revival: Alex's Album*), B, P, *Vol. III*, 123, *BOB*, 176

Bouquet Avec Trois Oiseaux, C, *BAQ*, 132, *BOB,* 73

Bowl of Flowers in a Rose Wreath (medallion), C, *BorMed*, Pullout

Bread and Wine, *BOB* (cover block), 205

Brenda's Rosebud Wreath, B, *Vol. I*, 127

Broken Wreath of Cherries, see Crown of Laurel

Broken Wreath of Roses, C, *BAQ*, 40, *BOB*, 17

Butterfly Medallion Center, B, *SWAW*, 46

Butterfly Medallion Outline, B, *SWAW*, 48

Cabin Fever Calicoes (from *Friendship's Offering*), B, P, *Vol. III*, 100, *BOB*, 166

Cactus Flower, *DABAQ*, 85

Canopy of Heaven Border, C, *Vol. II*, 172 (Pattern #33), *BOB*, 137

★Carnations (from *Classic Revival: Alex's Album*), B, P, *Vol. III*, 119, *BOB II*, 136

Central Medallion (set for Basket with Blooms, Bird and Bible with Triple-Bowed Garland Borders), C, *SWAW*, 36

Cherry Wreath with Bluebirds I and II, C, *BAQ*, 62, *BOB*, 33

Cherubs (from *Friendship's Offering*), B, P, *Vol. II*, 105, *BOB*, 168

★Christmas Cactus (from *Classic Revival: Alex's Album*), S, P, *Vol. III*, 125, *BOB II,* 140

Christmas Cactus I, C, *BAQ*, 33, *BOB*, 14

★Circular Sprays of Flowers, S, *BAQ*, 39, *BOB I*, 31

Clipper Ship, C, *BAQ*, 156, *BOB*, 93

Cornucopia II, C, *BAQ*, 140

★Cornucopia III, C, *Vol. III*, 134, *BOB II*, 149

Cornucopia with Fruits and Acorns, C, *SWAW*, 63, *BOB*, 213

Crossed Laurel Sprays, C, *Vol. I*, 122

Crossed Pine Cones and Rosebuds, C, *Vol. II*, 114, *BOB*, 106

Crossed Sprays of Flowers, C, *BAQ*, 52

Crown of Laurel (Broken Wreath of Cherries), B, *Vol. I*, 138

Crown of Laurel with Rose, *BOB*, 201

Crown of Quilted Roses, B, *DA*, 80, *BOB*, 144

Crown of Ruched Roses, B, *DA*, 98, *BOB*, 146

Crown of Ten Penny Roses, B, *DA*, 78, *BOB*, 142

Dancing Grapevine Border, The, B, *BorMed*, 58

Devon Violets for Nana (from *Classic Revival: Alex's Album*), B, P, *Vol. III*, 121

Diagonal Bough of Apples, S, *BAQ*, 66, *BOB*, 37

Diagonal Floral Spray I, C, *BAQ*, 64, *BOB*, 35

Divine Guidance, B, *Vol. I*, 119

Dogtooth Border, C, *Vol. II*, 169 (Pattern #26), *BOB*, 134

Dogtooth Triangle Border I, C, *Vol. II*, 170 (Pattern #29), *BOB*, 135

Dogtooth Triangle Border II, C, *Vol. II*, 170 (Pattern #30), *BOB*, 135

★Double Hearts, C, P, *Vol. I*, 117, *Vol. III*, 119, *BOB II*, 136

★Dove and Lyre, S, *Vol. III*, 146, *BOB II*, 157

Dutch Bulbs a-Bloomin', Version I and II, T, *AP12*, 28–29

Dutch Bulbs a-Bloomin', Version III (Winding Rose), T, *AP12*, 30

Dutch Country Hearts (quilt), T, *AP12*, 59

★Eiffel Tower (from *Lindsay's Album*), B, P, *Vol. III*, 128, *BOB II*, 143

Eight-Pointed Star with Sprigs of Berries, C, *SWAW*, 56

Epergne of Fruit, C, *Vol. I*, 166

Epergne of Fruit III, C, *Vol. III*, 185, *BOB*, 193

Epergne of Fruit IV, C, *Vol. III*, 189, *BOB*, 197

E Plurubus Unum: Eagles and Oaks (from *Classic Revival: Alex's Album*), B, P, *Vol. III*, 118

★Family Pets (from *Remembrance II*), B, P, *Vol. III*, 130, *BOB II*, 145

Fancy Flowers, B, *DA*, 156, *BOB*, 158

Feathered Star, P, S, *Vol. I*, 120

Feather-Wreathed Album in a Rose Lyre (medallion), C, *BorMed*, Pullout

Feather-Wreathed Heart, B, *Vol. I*, 130

Feather-Wreathed Heart with Doves (Love), B, *Vol. I*, 128

★Five Borders and a Medallion, BOB, 133–136, *BOB II*, 112,121

★Flamingos (from *Lindsay's Album*), B, *Vol. III*, 128, *BOB II*, 143

Fleur-de-Lis I, P, C, *BAQ*, 23,

★Fleur-de-Lis II, P, S, *BAQ*, 23, *BOB II*, 20

Fleur-de-Lis III, P, B, *Vol. II*, 116

Fleur-de-Lis and Rosebuds, C, *SWAW*, 20

Fleur-de-Lis and Rose Medallion (from *Classic Revival: Alex's Album*), B, P, *Vol. III*, 113

★Fleur-de-Lis Medallion I, C, P, *BAQ*, 22, *BOB II*, 19

★Fleur-de-Lis Medallion II, B, *BAQ*, 42, *BOB*, 15, *BOB II*, 32

Fleur-de-Lis Variation (from *Classic Revival: Alex's Album*, two patterns), C, P, *Vol. III*, 126

Fleur-de-Lis with Folded Rosebuds II, B, *Vol. I*, 125

Fleur-de-Lis with Maple Leaves, *DABAQ*, 84

Fleur-de-Lis with Rosebuds III, B, *BAQ*, 34, *BOB*, 15

★Fleur-de-Lis with Rosebuds IV, B, *BAQ*, 35, *BOB II*, 28

Flower Basket, C, *SWAW*, 54

Flowers Around Friendship's Chain (from *Classic Revival: Alex's Album*), B, P, *Vol. III*, 121

★Flower-Wreathed Heart II, S, *DA*, 102, *BOB II*, 78

★Folk Art Basket of Flowers, C, *DA*, 116, *BOB II*, 86

★Folk Art Bird, S, *Vol. III*, 181, *BOB II*, 180

Folk Art Flower Wheel, C, *BAQ*, 29

Folk Art Vase of Flowers, C, *BAQ*, 68, *BOB*, 39

Four-Ribbon Wreath, C, *BAQ*, 168

Friendship Is a Sheltering Tree Picture, S, T, *AP12*, 51

Friendship's Offering, C, *SWAW*, 26

Friendship's Offering Border, C, *BorMed*, 71

Garden Cats (from *Friendship's Offering*), B, P, *Vol. III*, 107, *BOB*, 169

Geranium Bird, S, *Vol. III*, 165, *BOB*, 185

George Washington's Redbud (from *Classic Revival: Alex's Album*), B, P, *Vol. III*, 113

★Goose Girl, S, *Vol. II*, 136, *BOB II*, 62

★Goose Girl Milking, B, *Vol. II*, 119, *BOB II*, 53

★Grape-flanked Urn of Fruit, *BOB II*, 209

Grapevine Border, *DA*, Pullout

Grapevine Lyre Wreath, B, *BAQ*, 56, *BOB*, 29

Grapevine Wreath, B, *Vol. II*, 156

Grape Vine Wreath, C, *SWAW*, 50

★Grapevine Wreath II, S, *BAQ*, 36, *BOB II*, 29

★Great Grandma May Ross Hamilton's Scottish Thistle (from *Classic Revival: Alex's Album*), B, P, *Vol. III*, 120, *BOB II*, 137

★Half-Wreath of Blooms from Mrs. Mann's Quilt, C, *Vol. III*, 169, *BOB II*, 172

Hammock and Bow Border, C, *Vol. II* (Pattern #23), 165, *BOB*, 130

★Hans Christian Andersen's Danish Hearts, B, P, *Vol. II*, 112, *BOB II*, 50

★Heart Medallion Frame, B, *Vol. II*, 118, *BOB II*, 51

Heart of Country (small quilt), T, *AP12*, 58

Hearts and Crosses (small quilt), *AP12*, 69

Hearts and Hands (from *Friendship's Offering*), B, P, *Vol. III*, 101

★Hearts and Hands in a Feather Wreath, B, *Vol. II*, 120, *BOB II*, 54

Hearts and Flowers Border Quilt, P, T, *AP12*, 72

★Hearts and Swans, B, P, *Vol. III*, 104, *BOB II*,128

★Hearts and Swans I and II, B, P, *BAQ*, 27, *BOB II*, 23

★Hearts and Tulips, C, *BAQ*, 30, *BOB*, 13, *BOB II*, 138

Hearts and Tulips (from *Classic Revival: Alex's Album*), C, P, *Vol. III*, 122

Heart-Shaped Garland, C, *SWAW*, 38

Heartsong (small quilt), *AP12*, 66

★Heart Wreath of Acorns, B, *BOB II*, 186

★Heart Wreath of Cherries, B, *BOB II*, 188

★Heart Wreath of Roses, B, *BOB II*, 184

★Heart Wreath of Tulips, B, *BOB II*, 190

Heart Wreathed with Vine, C, P, *SWAW*, 38

Heart Wreath with Buds, *DABAQ*, 87

Herald Angels, C, *SWAW*, 40

Holly, Bows, and Berries (small quilt), T, *AP12*, 60

Holly, Laurel, and Hearts (placemats), T, *AP12*, 55

Holly-Wreathed Apron, T, *AP12*, 49

Home-Grown Rose Border, The, C, *BorMed*, 13

Honey Bee Hearts (small quilt), T, *AP12*, 65

Hospitality, S, *Vol. I*, 124

Hunting Scene, C, *SWAW*, 14

Inscribed Wreath of Roses (medallion), *DA*, Pullout

★Intertwined Crown of Flowers—Stem Layout, *BOB II*, 201

I Promised You a Rose Garden, B, *DA*, 75, *BOB*, 139

★Ivy Basket with Bow, B, *DA*, 124, *BOB II*, 94

Jeanne's Grapevine Wreath, B, *Vol. II*, 156, *BOB*, 125

Jeannie's Blue Baltimore Basket, B, *DA*, 136

★Jeannie's Iris, Pansy, and Pleated Flowers Basket, B, *DA*, 128, *BOB II*, 98

Joy Nichol's Peacock, B, *Vol. II*, 148, *BOB*, 117

Joy Nichol's Rose of Sharon, B, *Vol. II*, 115, *BOB*, 107

★Kangaroos (from *Friendship's Offering*), B, P, *Vol. III*, 94, *BOB II*, 122

Katya's Album (quilt), P, S, T, *AP12*, 70

Katya's Angels (Christmas tree skirt), T, *AP12*, 57

★Kaye's Ribbon Basket, B, *DA*, 163, *BOB II*, 111

Lacy Heart Apron, T, *AP12*, 49

★Landon Bears Football Team (from *Classic Revival: Alex's Album*), B, P, *Vol. III*, 122, *BOB II*, 138

Laurel and Swag Border, *DABAQ*, 69

Leafy Border, *DA*, Pullout

★Lindsay as a Young Gymnast (from *Lindsay's Album*), B, P, *Vol. III*, 129, *BOB II*, 144

Linked Poseys, *DABAQ*, 86

★Lovely Lane's Grapevine Wreath, C, *DA*, 104, *BOB II*, 80

Love, see Feather-Wreathed Heart with Doves

Love Birds on a Rose Perch, S, *Vol. III*, 173, *BOB*, 189

Lyre *Scherenschnitte*, B, P, *BAQ*, 50, *BOB*, 12
Lyre with Laurel Sprays I, C, *BAQ*, 50, *BOB*, 23
Lyre with Wreath and Bird, C, *SWAW*, 22
Lyre with Wreath, Bird, and Crown, C, *BAQ*, 136, *BOB*, 77
Lyre Wreath, B, *Vol. I*, 150
Maryland Manor House, C, *BAQ*, 144, *BOB*, 85
Melodies of Love, C, *BAQ*, 124, *BOB*, 65
Mirrored-Ribbon Border, The, C, *BorMed*, 23
Mrs. Mann's Quilt Border, *DA*, Pullout
Numsen Bouquet I: Foliage, B, *DA*, 148
Numsen Family Lyre, C, *Vol. II*, 124, *BOB*, 111
Oak Leaves and Acorns—for Longevity (from *Classic Revival: Alex's Album*), B, P, *Vol. III*, 116, *BOB*, 173
Oak Leaves and Reel (quilt), P, T, *AP12*, 74
Palmetto Border (from *Classic Revival: Alex's Album*), C, P, *Vol. III*, 115
Palmetto-Tied Laurel Garland Border, The, C, *BorMed*, 63
Papercuts, 26 unnamed patterns from *Friendship's Offering*, B, P, *Vol. III*, 94–110
Patriotic Eagle, C, *SWAW*, 24, *BOB*, 207
Peace, Love, and Liberty (patriotic pillow), T, *AP12*, 53
Peacock Pastorale, C, *BAQ*, 160, *BOB*, 97
*Pedestal Basket with Handle, B, *DA*, 161, *BOB II*, 110
Peony and Hammock Border, C, *Vol. II* (Pattern #22), 162, *BOB*, 127
Peony Center (medallion, 4-block repeat), possibly B, *BAQ*, 80, *BOB*, 51
*Pineapple (from *Classic Revival: Alex's Album*), S, P, *Vol. III*, 112, *BOB II*, 133
Pineapples, C, *SWAW*, 42
*Pinecones for Maine (from *Classic Revival: Alex's Album*), B, P, *Vol. III*, 124, *BOB II*, 139
Promises Picture, P, S, T, *AP12*, 52
Redbird Lyre, S, *BAQ*, 46, *BOB*, 21
*Red Bird on a Passion Flower Branch, S, *Vol. III*, 177, *BOB II*, 176
*Red Vases and Red Flowers, B, *BAQ*, 31, *BOB II*, 26
Red Woven Basket of Flowers, S, *Vol. I*, 162
*Regal Bird Amidst the Roses, B, *DA*, 132, *BOB II*, 102
Reverse Feather Plume Border, *DABAQ*, 69
*Ribbonwork Basket for *Broderie Perse* Blooms, B, *DA*, 163, *BOB II*, 111
*Rick Rack Roses, B, *DA*, 100, *BOB II*, 76
Ring with Holly (from *Classic Revival: Alex's Album*), S, P, *Vol. III*, 123
Rita Kelstrom's Round Basket, B, *DA*, 160, *BOB*, 162
Rosebud Border, *DA*, Pullout
Rosebud Wreathed Heart, B, *Vol. II*, 132, *BOB*, 113
*Rose Cornucopias, S, *BAQ*, 48, *BOB II*, 34
Rose Lyre II, S, *BAQ*, 44, *BOB*, 19
*Rose Medallion, B, P, *Vol. III*, 120, *BOB II*, 137
Rose of Sharon, T, *SWAW*, 62, *BOB*, 217
*Rose of Sharon II, C, *BAQ*, 28, *BOB II*, 24
Rose of Sharon III, C, *BAQ*, 38, *BOB*, 16
Rose of Sharon Border, The, C, *BorMed*, 19
Roses Are Red, B, *DA*, 74, *BOB*, 138
Roses for Hans Christian Andersen, B, *BAQ*, 54, *BOB*, 27
Rose Wreath with Red Birds, C, *Vol. I*, 144
*Ruched Ribbon Rose Lyre II, B, *Vol. III*, 132, *BOB II*, 147
Ruched Rose Lyre, B, *Vol. I*, 154
Ruffled Border, C, *Vol. II* (Pattern #28), 170, *BOB*, 135
Scalloped Border, C, *Vol. II* (Pattern #24), 168, *BOB*, 133
Scalloped Border, C, *Vol. II* (Pattern #31), 171, *BOB*, 136
*Scalloped Epergne of Fruit, C, *BAQ*, 120, *BOB II*, 46
Send Flowers (placemats), T, *AP12*, 56
Silhouette Wreath, B, *Vol. I*, 134
Simpler Palmetto Frame (from *Classic Revival: Alex's Album*), C, P, *Vol. III*, 111
*Sometimes Take Tea (from *Bonnie's Album*), B, P, *Vol. III*, 127, *BOB II*, 142
Squared Grapevine Wreath, C, *Vol. II*, 122, *BOB*, 109
Square Wreath with Fleur-de-Lis and Rosebuds, C, *Vol. II*, 113, *BOB*, 105
*Squared Wreath of Embroidered Flowers, B, *BOB II*, 200

Star of Hearts, B, P, *Vol. I* 121
Star of Hearts (quilt), T, *AP12*, 77
Steamship Captain Russell, The, C, *SWAW*, 28
Stepped Border (four steps), C, *Vol. II*, (Pattern #25), 168, *BOB*, 133
Stepped Border (six steps), C, *Vol. II*, (Pattern #27), 169, *BOB*, 134
Stepped Border (three steps), C, *Vol. II*, (Pattern #32), 171, *BOB*, 136
Straight Rose-Vine Border, The, C, *BorMed*, Pullout
Strawberry Clusters in the Shape of a Cross within a Circle, C, *SWAW*, 52
*Strawberry Wreath II, S, *BAQ*, 37, *BOB II*, 30
*Strawberry Wreath III, C, *Vol. III*, 142, *BOB II*, 153
Sugar Cookies (small quilt), T, *AP12*, 63
Sunbonnet Sue, Mini-(small quilt), T, *AP12*, 62
Sunflower (from *Classic Revival: Alex's Album*), C, P, *Vol. III*, 115
Swag and Blossom Border, *DABAQ*, 68
Sweet Doves of Liberty (patriotic pillow), T, *AP12*, 54
Sweet Gum for the Severn River (from *Classic Revival: Alex's Album*), B, P, *Vol. III*, 116
Sweetheart Rose Lyre, B or C, *Vol. I*, 132
*Sylvia's *Wycinanki*, B, P, *BAQ*, 26, *BOB II*, 22
Symbolic Fountain, C, *BAQ*, 148, *BOB*, 89
Tasseled-Ribbon Swag Border, C, *BorMed*, 26
Tender Tulips, *DABAQ*, 83
Texas Treasures, B, *DA*, 152, *BOB*, 154
*Theorem-style Urn of Flowers, C, *BOB II*, 213
*Theorem-style Urn of Fruit, C, *BOB II*, 205
*Tiptoe Through My Tulips, B, P, *Vol. III*, 131, *BOB II*, 146
Token of Gratitude, A, S, *Vol. I*, 136
Tree of Life, S, *Vol. III*, 153, *BOB*, 181
Triple-Bowed Garland Borders, C, *SWAW*, 34
Tropical Bird in a Bush, C, *BAQ*, 152
*Tropical Boating, S, *Vol. II*, 144, *BOB II*, 70
Trumpet Vine, C, P, *SWAW*, 44
*Turtle Hill (from *Classic Revival: Alex's Album*), B, P, *Vol. III*, 117, *BOB II*, 135
Twining Blooms and Baskets (quilt), T, *AP12*, 78
$200,000 Tulips, C, *Vol. I*, 123
*Unadorned Victorian Basket of Flowers, C, *DA*, 110, *BOB II*, 84
Updegraf Basket, Book, and Bird, C, *Vol. II*, 152, *BOB*, 121
Urn, T, 218
*Varietal Botanical I B, P, *Vol. III*, 96, *BOB II*, 123
*Varietal Botanical II, B, P, *Vol. III*, 97, *BOB II*, 124
*Varietal Botanical III, B, P, *Vol. III*, 98, *BOB II*, 125
*Varietal Botanical IV, B, P, *Vol. III*, 98, *BOB II*, 125
*Varietal Botanical V, B, P, *Vol. III*, 102, *BOB II*, 126
*Varietal Botanical VI, B, P, *Vol. III*, 103, *BOB II*, 127
*Varietal Botanical VII, B, P, *Vol. III*, 103, *BOB II*, 127
*Varietal Botanical IX, B, P, *Vol. III*, 106, *BOB II*, 129
*Varietal Botanical X, B, P, *Vol. III*, 106, *BOB II*, 129
*Varietal Botanical XI, B, P, *Vol. III*, 108, *BOB II*, 130
*Varietal Botanical XI, B, P, *Vol. III*, 109 *BOB II*, 131
*Varietal Botanical XII, B, P, *Vol. III*, 110, *BOB II*, 132
*Varietal Botanical XIII, C, P, *Vol. III*, 114, *BOB II*, 134
*Varietal Botanical XIV, S, P, *Vol. III*, 124, *BOB II*, 139
*Varietal Botanical XV, S, P, *Vol. III*, 125, *BOB II*, 140
*Varietal Fleur-de-Lis I, B, P, *Vol. III*, 94 *BOB II*, 122
*Varietal Fleur-de-Lis II, B, P, *Vol. III*, 96, *BOB II*, 123
*Varietal Fleur-de-Lis III, B, P, *Vol. III*, 97, *BOB II*, 124
*Varietal Fleur-de-Lis IV, B, P, *Vol. III*, 99, *BOB II*, 124
*Varietal Fleur-de-Lis V, B, P, *Vol. III*, 109 *BOB II*, 131
*Varietal Fleur-de-Lis VI, B, P, *Vol. III*, 110, *BOB II*, 132
*Varietal Fleur-de-Lis VII, C, P, *Vol. III*, 114, *BOB II*, 134
*Varietal Fleur-de-Lis VIII, S, P, *Vol. III*, 126, *BOB II*, 140
*Varietal Fleur-de-Lis IX, C, P, *Vol. III*, 126, *BOB II*, 140
Vase of Full-Blown Roses I, S, *DA*, 106, *BOB*, 148
Vase of Full-Blown Roses II: Rose Amphora, S, *Vol. III*, 138
Vase of Full-Blown Roses IV, C, *BAQ*, 58
Vase of Roses I, C, *Vol. I*, 142
Vase with Floral Bouquet, Harp, Doves, and Bible, C, *SWAW*, 16
*Vase with Fruits and Flowers, C, *BAQ*, 60, *BOB II*, 36

Victorian Basket of Flowers II, C, *BAQ*, 88
Victorian Basket of Flowers III, S, *Vol. III*, 157, *BOB*, 43, *BOB II*, 164
★Victorian Basket of Flowers IV, C, *BAQ*, 92, *BOB*, 59, *BOB II*, 38
★Victorian Basket V with Fruits and Flowers, C, *BAQ*, 112, *BOB II*, 42
★Victorian Favorite, C, *BAQ*, 32, *BOB II*, 27
Victorian Ribbon Basket with Wire Ribbon Roses, B, *DA*, 112, *BOB*, 150
Victorian Vase of Flowers I, C, *BAQ*, 116, *BOB*, 63
Victorian Vase of Flowers III, C, *BAQ*, 72
Victorian Weave Basket, B, *DA*, 160, *BOB*, 162
★Violins and Bows (from *Bonnie's Album*), B, P, *Vol. III*, 127, *BOB II*, 142
Washington Monument in Baltimore, C, *SWAW*, 58
★Waterfowling, S, *Vol. II*, 140, *BOB II*, 66
Welcome Home Picture/House Blessing, T, *AP12*, 50
Wheel of Hearts, C, P, *SWAW*, 64
Wilanna's Basket Garden, B, *DA*, 140
Wreath and Dove, C, *Vol. I*, 158
Wreath and Dove II, C, *BAQ*, 164, *BOB*, 101
Wreath of Cherries, S, *Vol. I*, 126
Wreath of Folded Ribbon Roses, B, *DA*, 76, *BOB*, 140
★Wreath of Hearts I and II, *Vol. I*, 140, *Vol. II*, 126, *BOB II*, 56
Wreath of Roses, C, *BAQ*, 41, *BOB*, 18
Wreath of Strawberry Leaves, C, *Vol. I*, 146
You Are Perfect, B, P, *Vol. I*, 118
You've Stolen My Heart! (quilt), T, *AP12*, 13

THE TECHNIQUES

Appliqué
 Baste-and-Turn, *Vol. I*, 76; *AP12*, 23; see also Seams Pre-Basted Under
 Broderie Perse, DA, 30
 Buttonhole, *Vol. I*, 99
 Complex Pattern, *BAQ*, 178
 Cut-away (Cutwork), *Vol. I*, 30; *AP12*, 16; see also Interrupted Cutwork; Unit Cutwork
 Cut-away with Freezer Paper on Top, *AP12*, 20
 Edge-Fused Padded, *DA*, 32
 English-Paper, *Vol. I*, 77; *AP12*, 24
 Freezer Paper and Paste, *Vol. I*, 78
 Freezer Paper Inside, *Vol. I*, 77; *AP12*, 24
 Freezer Paper Inside with Adhesive, *AP12*, 26
 Freezer Paper on Top (Onlaid), *Vol. I*, 40, 46; (Inlaid), *Vol. I*, 42, 46; (with Papercuts), *Vol. III*, 40
 Freezer Paper Ribbon Appliqué, *DA*, 33
 Fused with a Blanket-Stitch finish, *AP12*, 22
 Fused with a Buttonhole Stitch, *Vol. I*, 101
 Hand, *SWAW*, 55
 Inlaid, see Freezer Paper on Top; Reverse Appliqué
 Interrupted Cutwork, *Vol. I*, 60
 Layering *vs*. Abutting, *Vol. I*, 53
 Machine, *AP12*, 26, 63; *SWAW*, 55
 Naturalistic, *DA*, 49
 Needleturn, *Vol. I*, 52, 66; *AP12*, 21, 33
 Onlaid, see Freezer Paper on Top
 Overlay Appliqué (Flat or Stuffed), *DA*, 33
 Papercut, *Vol. III*, 38, see also Papercut Designs
 Reverse (Inlaid), *Vol. I*, 35, 79, *AP12*, 21
 Running Stitch, *Vol. I*, 65
 Seams Pre-Basted Under, *Vol. I*, 75; see also Baste-and-Turn
 Spray, *Vol. I*, 77; *AP12*, 25
 Straight-Edge, *Vol. I*, 47
 Template (Plastic), *Vol. I*, 78
 Unit Cutwork, *Vol. I*, 49, 55
 Yo-Yo, *Vol. I*, 79
Background Fabric, Marking the, *Vol. III*, 17
Baskets
 Bouquet Shape, *DA*, 49
 (Braided) Ribbonwork, *DA*, 31
 Cut-Away, *DA*, 36
 Latticework with Turned-Bias Stems, *DA*, 34–35
 Monochromatic, *DA*, 47
 Paperfolding for Shape, *DA*, 48
 Pleat-Bordered, *DA*, 43
 Raw-Edged Bias Strips, *DA*, 33
 Ribbon, *DA*, 24
 Solid-Shape (Whole-Cloth), *DA*, 37
 Weaving, *DA*, 13, 24, 47, 49
Bindings
 Mock, *DABAQ*, 75
 Updegraf (Scalloped), *DABAQ*, 76
 Beehive, *DABAQ*, 77
Border Patterns
 Designing, *DABAQ*, 39
 Dogtooth, *Vol. I*, 47; *Vol. II*, 78
 Transferring, *BorMed*, 11
Broderie Perse, DA, 30
Centers for Flowers
 French Knot, *DA*, 57
 Rolled Rose, *DA*, 57
 Wool Turkeywork, *DA*, 57
 Yo-Yo, *DA*, 56
Circles, Perfect, *Vol. I*, 73; see also Berries; Grapes
Designing
 Balancing, *Vol. III*, 43
 Block Arrangement, *DABAQ*, 27
 Blocks, *DABAQ*, 29
 Borders, *DABAQ*, 39
  Buildings, *Vol. II*, 35
  Cannibalized Large Prints, *DA*, 41
  Classic Sets, *DABAQ*, 10, 15; *Vol. II*, 75
  Medallions, *DABAQ*, 27, 37
  Ornamenting, *Vol. III*, 41
  People, *Vol. II*, 33
Dogtooth Border, *Vol. II*, 78
Dyeing, Microwave, *DA*, 39
Flowers, see also Centers for, Rosebuds, Roses
 Asters, *DA*, 42
 Bell Flowers, *DA*, 46
 Bluebells, *DA*, 70
 Botanical Basics, *DA*, 13
 Camelia, Ruching a Ribbon, *DA*, 69
 Christmas Cactus Bud, *DA*, 71
 Dahlias, Wire Ribbon, *DA*, 29
 Daisies, *DA*, 42
 Foxgloves, *DA*, 70
 Finishing, *DA*, 57
 Gathered and Rolled Strip Flowers, *DA*, 18
 Gathered Petal, *DA*, 45
 Lilacs, Gathered, *DA*, 32
 Lilies of the Valley, *DA*, 70
 Orchard Blossoms, *DA*, 41
 Pansies, Wire Ribbon, *DA*, 28
 Peony Bud, Puff-Centered, *DA*, 70
 Petals-on-a-String, *DA*, 60
 Pleated, *DA*, 59
 Posies, Red Wire Ribbon, *DA*, 71
 Primroses, *DA*, 70
 Primroses, Wire Ribbon, *DA*, 29
 Rick Rack Blooms, *DA*, 59, 63
 Ruched, *DA*, 63
 Template Free, *Vol. I*, 62
 Violets, *DA*, 41
Fruit
 Berries as Fillers, *Vol. III*, 24
 Berries, Stuffed, *Vol. I*, 71
 Blackberries, *Vol. III*, 24
 Blueberries, *Vol. III*, 25

Cantaloupe, *Vol. III*, 23
Fabric Choices, *Vol. III*, 32
Grapes, Perfect, *Vol. I*, 72; *AP12*, 31
Greengage Plum, *Vol. III*, 27
Muskmelon, see Fruit: Pineapple
Olallaberries, *Vol. III*, 21
Oranges, Seville, *Vol. III*, 26
Peach, *Vol. III*, 27
Pineapple, *Vol. III*, 18–21
Raspberries, *Vol. III*, 25
Stem-Well Circle, *Vol. III*, 33
Watermelon (Stenciling), *Vol. III*, 31
Gauging, *Vol. III*, 19
Cantaloupe, *Vol. III*, 23
Olallaberries, *Vol. III*, 21
Pineapple, *Vol. III*, 18–21
Ink Embellishments, see Writing
Invisible Nylon Thread, Handsewing with,
DA, 21
Leaves
Crack'n Peel, *DA*, 25
Doubled and Bonded, *DA*, 22
Embellishments, *DA*, 55
Finishing, *DA*, 23
Freezer Paper Ribbon Appliqué, *DA*, 33
Folded Ribbon, *DA*, 22
Fringed Ferns, *DA*, 42
Gathered, *DA*, 60
Needleturning, *Vol. I*, 71; *AP12*, 33
Pineapple, *Vol. III*, 19
Seamed and Turned, *DA*, 22
Simple Tucked, *DA*, 22
Split, *DA*, 55
Straight-Stitched, *DA*, 53
Light Sources, *Vol. III*, 33
Medallions
Acorn and Oak Leaf Frame, *Vol. II*, 32
Designing, *DABAQ*, 29, 37
Heart Medallion Frame, *Vol. II*, 31
Papercut Frame, *Vol. II*, 30
Papercut Designs, *Vol. III*, 38
Design Formula, *Vol. III*, 54
Eight-Repeat Block, *Vol. III*, 44, 45, 47
Asymmetry, *Vol. III*, 52
"Found" Figurative Motif, *Vol. III*, 52
Main Design Between Triangle Base and Hypoteneuse,
Vol. III, 50
Main Design on Hypoteneuse, *Vol. III*, 48
Main Design on Side and Hypoteneuse, *Vol. III*, 51
Two-Color, *Vol. III*, 49
Medallion-Centered Frame, *Vol. II*, 30
Personalizing, *Vol. III*, 55
Representational, *Vol. III*, 46
Two-Repeat Block, *Vol. III*, 38, 41
Pattern
Bridges, *Vol. I*, 39, 52
Transferring, *Vol. I*, 21; *BorMed*, 11
Photocopying, *Vol. III*, 17
Tracing, *Vol. III*, 17
Portrait Epergnes, *Vol. III*, 35
Pressing, Starched, *DA*, 50
Print Windows, *DA*, 26; *Vol. III*, 33
Ribbons, *DA*, 12
Basket, *DA*, 24
Camelia, Ruching, *DA*, 69
Dahlias, Wire Ribbon, *DA*, 29
Folded Ribbon Flower, *AP12*, 32
Folded Ribbon Leaves, *DA*, 22
Painting, *DA*, 59
Pansies, Wire Ribbon *DA*, 28
Posies, Red Wire Ribbon, *DA*, 71

Primroses, Wire Ribbon, *DA*, 29
Roses, Rolled Wire Ribbon, *DA*, 18, 19–21
Rosebuds
Folded II, *Vol. I*, 55
Folded Ribbon Flower *AP12*, 32
Tucked-Circle, *DA*, 36
Roses
Charlotte Jane Whitehill (Versions I, II, & III), *DA*, 38
Cutwork, *Vol. I*, 62
Embellishments (for Moss Roses), *DA*, 27
Embroidered Rose Hairs, *Vol. I*, 59
Floribunda, *DA*, 69
Folded Rose (Wire Ribbon), *DA*, 21
Full-Blown Rose (Wire Ribbon), *DA*, 19
Layered, *Vol. I*, 62
Layered-Circle (Quarter), *DA*, 35
Many-Petaled (CJWhitehill III), DA, 39
Mrs. Numsen's I, *DA*, 61
Mrs. Numsen's II, *DA*, 66
Mrs. Numsen's III, *DA*, 68
Mrs. Numsen's Fringed Center, *DA*, 27
1920s, *DA*, 43
Nova (CJWhitehill II), *DA*, 39
Open Rose (Wire Ribbon) *DA*, 21
Quarter (layered-circle), *DA*, 35
Quilted, *DA*, 54
Rick Rack, *DA*, 58
Rolled Wire Ribbon, *DA*, 18
Ruching, *Vol. I*, 66; *DA*, 56
Centers for, *DA*, 56
Stuffed Silk, *Vol. I*, 60
Ruching, see also Flowers, Roses
Coin, *DA*, 64
Half, *DA*, 65
Heart-Monitor, *DA*, 64
Ribbon, *DA*, 69
Shell, *DA*, 64
Scherenschnitte, see Papercut Designs
Speed Stitching from the Back, *DA*, 35
Stems
Fine, *SWAW*, 55
Machine, *DA*, 52
Super, *Vol. I*, 73
Superfine, *Vol. I*, 69; *AP12*, 31; *DA*, 51, 52
Turned-Bias, *DA*, 34
Stem-Well Circle, *Vol. III*, 33
Stenciling, *Vol. III*, 29–34
Stitches
Blanket, *DA*, 30
Blind (a.k.a. Invisible, Ladder, Pumpkin, Jack-O'-Lantern, Slip,
Speed, or Hem), *Vol. I*, 40
Buttonhole, *Vol. I*, 99; *DA*, 30
Chain, *DA*, 36
Embellishments by Gwen LeLacheur, *DA*, 62
French Knot, *AP12*, 9; *Vol. III*, 25
Tack, *Vol. I*, 37
Threaded Straight-Stitch, *DA*, 36
Symbolism, Adding, *Vol. III*, 56
Templates
Asymmetrical *vs.* Symmetrical, *DA*, 27
Print Windows, *DA*, 26
Writing on Cloth, *Vol. I*, 44, 62; *AP12*, 26; *Vol. III*, 33
Banners, *Vol. II*, 24
Copperplate Hand Lettering, *Vol. II*, 21
Embellishments, *DA*, 70
For Fruit, *Vol. III*, 33
For Moss Roses, *DA*, 27
Engraved Signature Logos, *Vol. II*, 21
"Friendship" Logo, *Vol. I*, 141
"Love" Logo, *Vol. I*, 129
"Marriage" Logo, *Vol. I*, 151

Elly Sienkiewicz has written sixteen important needlework books on appliqué, from plain to fancy. Twelve of her books are on the Baltimore Album Quilts, eleven of them comprise the Baltimore Beauties and Beyond series, begun in 1989. Elly places a complex historical style—the Baltimore-style Album Quilts—within the grasp of every contemporary quiltmaker. She does this through clear patterns and techniques which demystify the construction process. Her leadership sustains this revival, now twenty years strong. In a linked fellowship, those who love this style have taken it to something closely related but clearly "beyond Baltimore."

Elly's path from career woman to stay-at-home mom of three, led her to become an early professional in the nascent quilt movement of early 1970s. Elly notes that her Wellesley College Class of 1964 is a "cusp generation"—women who as freshmen expected to live their mothers' 1950s societal ideal, but who were radically different by the time they graduated. Elly went on to the University of Pennsylvania to earn a Masters of Science degree and thence to teach high school for seven years. A history major with a lifetime love of needleart, Elly's traditionalist spirit desired to stay home once her children began to arrive. She was led to home-centered enterpises, eventually those relating to the burgeoning quilt industry. Her experiences ranged from quilting teacher to retail mail-order proprietress, to respected quiltmaker, to author and historian. Since 1996 she has presided over the annual Elly Sienkiewicz Appliqué Academy (www.EllySienkiewicz.com) now in Williamsburg, Virginia. Elly's devotion as a teacher, her patience, her concern for her students, and her love for quiltmaking have made her a cherished mentor. She lives in Washington, DC, with her husband, and whenever they return home, son Donald and wife Katya and children Ellie and Elias; son Alex and wife Holly, and daughter Katya. See Elly's website for her teaching schedule.

Fifteen books by Elly Sienkiewicz

Appliqué 12 Borders and Medallions

Appliqué 12 Easy Ways!

Appliqué Paper Greetings!

Baltimore Album Legacy

Baltimore Album Quilts

Baltimore Album Revival

Baltimore Beauties and Beyond, Vol. I

Baltimore Beauties and Beyond, Vol. II

Design a Baltimore Album Quilt

Dimensional Appliqué

Fancy Appliqué

Papercuts and Plenty, Baltimore Beauties and Beyond, Vol. II

Romancing Ribbons into Flowers

Spoken Without a Word

The Best of Baltimore Beauties

The Best of Baltimore Beauties, Vol. II

For a complete listing of C&T titles send for a free catalog from:

C&T Publishing, Inc.
P.O. Box 1456
Lafayette, CA 94549
800-284-1114
http://www.ctpub.com
email:ctinfo@ctpub.com

For Quilting Supplies contact:

Cotton Patch Mail Order
3405 Hall Lane, Dept. CTB
Lafayette, Ca 94549
email: quiltusa@yahoo.com
Web: www.quiltusa.com
800-835-4418
925-283-7883